The Federal Reserve Conspiracy

By

Eustace Mullins

ISBN: 978-1-63923-229-1

Printed: June 2022

Cover Art By: Amit Paul

Published and Distributed By:
Lushena Books
607 Country Club Drive, Unit E
Bensenville, IL 60106
www.lushenabooksinc.com/books

ISBN: 978-1-63923-229-1

The Federal Reserve Conspiracy

By

Eustace Mullins

Published by

Christian Educational Assn.

Union, New Jersey

1954

PREFACE

In the fall of 1949 I went to the Library of Congress to get material for a newspaper article about the Federal Reserve Board of Governors. What I expected to be a week's labor turned into a lengthy research job of nineteen months, for I discovered, in my initial inquiry, that there existed not one narrative account of the origins and activities of this powerful organization. Consequently, the majority of my information was gathered piecemeal from a vast number of periodicals, ranging from popular magazines such as the Saturday Evening Post to the exclusive bankers' magazine, The Economist.

The standard works on the Federal Reserve System, almost entirely abstruse and technical works on economics, I found of little practical value. Even in the matter of acceptances, the usual textbooks contained no information upon such an important item in America's economic history as the changeover from the open-book system of credit to the acceptance system, which has wrought such vast changes in our practice of commerce, and for this information I found only one source, a few pamphlets published by the American Acceptance Council from 1915 to 1928. It is, then, little wonder that the student with a Master's Degree in Economics from one of the better universities will see here for the first time material which should have been before him in his elementary courses.

The birthplace of the Federal Reserve Act, Jekyl Island, is now operated as a public park by the State of Georgia, but the tourist will find no plaque there commemorating the event. This is not so much an oversight on the part of the park officials as it is a triumph for the more than adequate publicists of the Federal Reserve Board, who have perpetuated the comfortable fiction that the Act was born in the halls of Congress, the product of the minds of Carter Glass and Woodrow Wilson. It is the writer's hope that this and many similar fictions will not long survive the publication of this work.

E. MULLINS.

I wish to thank my fellow-members of the staff of the Library of Congress, whose very kind suggestions, assistance, and co-operation have made this book possible. I particularly wish to thank Mr. Luther Evans, Librarian of Congress, Col. Willard Webb of the Stack and Reader Division, and many other employees who have extended me every courtesy in the preparation of this work.

Eustace Mullins

Chapter One
NELSON ALDRICH

On the night of November 22, 1910, a crowd of newspaper reporters gathered at the Hoboken, New Jersey, railway station. They had been tipped off that some very highly-placed people were coming over to Hoboken from New York City to board a train and go away on a secret mission. What the mission might be, or who the personages involved, none of them knew, but they were certain that an extremely important event was in the making. Senator Nelson Aldrich entered the station. Here was their proof. The reporters gathered around him. He was always good copy, although he was noted for his brusqueness and the difficulty of getting a story from him. This was due to his tieup with the powerful Rubber Trust and the Tobacco Trust. As one of the coalition of five Republican Senators then ruling the Senate, Aldrich had used his elective position to enact a series of tariffs and laws favorable to his own interests, and had been denounced many times for his callous disregard of his oath of office as he devoted his power to the program of international financier.

Aldrich had recently returned from Europe with the National Monetary Commission, of which he was head. This was a Commission appointed by Congress in response to public feeling against big bankers after the artificial Panic of 1907. The commission had been charged to make a thorough study of financial practices before formulating banking and currency reform legislation for Congress It was pointed out at the time that such legislation seemed unlikely to offer genuine reform under the leadership of a man with Aldrich's known sympathies and employment but Congress was blithely impervious to this criticism.

Senator Aldrich and the National Monetary Commission had spent nearly two years touring Europe at the American taxpayer's expense. He and his entourage had dissipated more than three hundred thousand dollars of public money, although they had been wined and dined by all the important European financiers and seemed to live off the land wherever they travelled. Since his return to this country, Senator Aldrich had made no effort to report to Congress the outcome of his trip, nor had he as yet offered any ideas as to banking reform. The nation waited for him to provide a cure for the recurring financial panics which had upset business and small fortunes continually since the Civil War. He had not come to any definite plan for such a cure.

With Senator Aldrich was A. Piatt Andrew, professional economist and Assistant Secretary of the Treasury, who had travelled with Aldrich to Europe as Special Assistant to the National Monetary Commission. They were followed by Aldrich's private secretary,

Shelton, and reporters with a number of pieces of luggage. Evidently they were going away for an extended time. The crowd of reporters, representing most of the great New York dailies, were convinced that the secret mission must have some connection with the proposed financial reform, and clustered aggressively around Aldrich, demanding a story.

Aldrich was accustomed to dealing with reporters, and walked past them without answering any of the questions shouted at him, nor did his companions so much as look up at the newsmen. They entered Aldrich's private car at the end of the train, and the shades were immediately drawn over the windows. The reporters were left to speculate with each other on the possible destination of the legislators.

Their curiosity was increased when they saw coming into the station two more bankers, followed by a group of porters. Here was Frank Vanderlip, a stocky, genial man who had risen from working as a farmhand to become President of the National City Bank of New York, the most powerful bank in this country, representing the Rockefeller oil interests and the railroad systems owned by the banking house of Kuhn, Loeb Company. The National City Bank had large interests in South America, and had been charged in 1898 with getting the United States to go to war with Spain. At any rate, the National City Bank came out of the Spanish-American War as the proprietor of Cuba's sugar industry.

With Vanderlip was the austere Henry P. Davison, senior partner of J. P. Morgan Company, and Charles D. Norton, President of Morgan's First National Bank of New York. These three financiers were dominant in the small group of New York Bankers which had been accused of controlling the entire money and credit of the United States. In response to the reporter's question, Mr. Vanderlip declared that they were only going away for a quiet weekend in the country.

These men controlled the oil, railroads, communications, and heavy industry of this country. What plan of action brought them skulking out of New York to board a private train on the other side of the river? Men as powerful as these had no reason to hide their comings and goings, and in the past they had been openly scornful of public opinion and public interest. No large new enterprise could be undertaken without coming to one or more of these men, and they saw to it that their advice and aid were well recompensed. They elected Congressmen, appointed Judges, and bought and sold newspapers and publishing houses whenever they needed a job done. One of their number had once earned a sort of fame by exclaiming "The public be damned!" It was not in character that they should cloak themselves in mystery.

The reporters had the same luck with these bankers that they had

had with Aldrich, and watched their story disappear into Aldrich's private car. The next figure to appear was not so well known to them. This was Paul Moritz Warburg, a German immigrant who had been in this country less than eight years, but who had so availed himself of the privileges of this land of opportunity that he was already a partner in the banking house of Kuhn, Loeb Company, New York, at a salary of five hundred thousand dollars a year. His family house of M. M. Warburg Company, of Hamburg and Amsterdam, was the chief German representative of the great European banking family, the Rothschilds. Liberal amounts of Rothschild funds had enabled Jacob Schiff to purchase a partnership in Kuhn, Loeb Company and less than twenty years later achieve an unchallenged domination over the large railway systems of the United States.

Paul Warburg had not devoted much attention to business since he arrived in this country. Instead, he had spent much of his time writing and lecturing on the subject of monetary reform. This seemed to be in direct conflict with his personal interests and the interests of his employers, for a genuine monetary reform would certainly reduce their profits and power, but his work along these lines brought him an increased salary and even more time to advocate banking legislation which would set up a central bank in the United States similar to those of Europe. Warburg was already known as the "banking brain" of New York, and commanded large audiences among the city bankers when he spoke at the meetings of the Chamber of Commerce or other bankers' fraternal groups.

With Warburg was Benjamin Strong, who had come to prominence on Wall Street during the Panic of 1907 as an able lieutenant of J. P. Morgan, when he demonstrated his ability to carry out orders. This was a money panic which had been called by Morgan to wipe out the competition of the Heinze-Morse group in the banking, shipping, and iron industries. Strong's appearance as companion of Warburg was no accident, for the J. P. Morgan interests and Kuhn, Loeb interests had formed an alliance in 1901, known as the Northern Securities Company which dominated the country ever since. This alliance had put Theodore Roosevelt in as President of the United States in 1904 to delay the prosecution of the Northern Securities Company by the Department of Justice. Roosevelt was successful in doing this, and the Morgan-Kuhn-Loeb alliance was able to work out a more complicated and less vulnerable system. For this work, Roosevelt was given the name of "trust-buster." *

*Northern Securities was the consolidation of the Rothschild Empire in America, J. P. Morgan and Company having become international agency in 1869, when J. P. Morgan and Anthony Drexel went to London and concluded an agreement with N. M. Rothschild Company that J. P. Morgan Company would henceforth act as their agent. Thus Drexel Company of Philadelphia, J. P. Morgan Company of New York, Grenfell and Company, of London, and Morgan Harjes and Company of Paris transacted Rothschild business after 1869, and the Rothschilds were able to hide under a less known name. J. P. Morgan had been chosen for this high honor because of the affair of the Hall carbines during the civil war, when he swindled

Warburg and Strong were silent as the others, and the reporters watched the train leave the station without so much as a quote from any of the bankers. They returned to their papers with nothing more than a few paragraphs on the mysterious departure of the financiers from New York, but not a single metropolitan daily carried the story. The city editors wisely ignored the event.

The first public reference to the mysterious mission appeared some six years later, three years after the Federal Reserve Act had been passed and was in operation. This was an article by E. C. Forbes in Frank Leslie's magazine, a feature in praise of Paul Warburg which incidentally told a story called "Jekyl Island", giving the first revelation of what happened in November, 1910. Bit by bit, Forbes' account was enlarged upon during the next thirty years, in statements and biographies of the principal characters, until the entire story had come out.

Aldrich's private car, which had left Hoboken Station with drawn shades, had taken the financiers to Jekyl Island, Georgia, to the Jekyl Island Hunt Club, a very exclusive club owned by J. P. Morgan and a small group of influential New York bankers. The club was very isolated, and was used as a comfortable retreat far from the cares of the New York money market. Its advantageous location made it much in demand for pursuits other than hunting, and on such occasions members of the club were informed that they should not appear there for a certain number of days. When Aldrich's group left New York, the club's members had been notified that the club would be occupied for the next two weeks.

The Aldrich group was not interested at this time in hunting. They had come to Jekyl Island to get a lot of work done, and they wanted to do that work in absolute secrecy. For that reason, the customary attendants at the club were given two week vacations, and new servants brought in for this occasion. The Aldrich group felt that it was imperative that their identity be kept secret, and allowed no visitors during the next two weeks. They were so anxious to prevent any knowledge of their mission leaking out that they never used last names, calling each other by their first names only, such as Henry, Ben, and Paul.

This proved to be so satisfactory for all concerned that it was made more formal after their return to New York, when they organized the "first-name club" and limited its membership to those who had been on Jekyl Island.

Why all this secrecy? Why this thousand-mile trip in a closed railway car to a remote hunting club? The Aldrich group went there

his own government by selling to the Union Army from a Federal arsenal carbines which the Army had condemned. The affair has been thoroughly written up in Gustavus Myers' "History of the Great American Fortunes." Also J. P. Morgan's father, Julius S. Morgan, was a partner of George Peabody and Company, the financial agents of the Federal Government in London during the Civil War, and as such, had acted in the interests of the Rothschilds also documented by Myers.

to write the banking and currency legislation which the National Monetary Commission had been ordered to prepare. At stake was the future control of the money and credit of the United States. If any monetary reform was passed by Congress which was not written by and for the New York bankers, their power would be ended. As the most technically-informed of the bankers, Paul Warburg was charged with doing most of the drafting of the plan. Senator Nelson Aldrich was there to see that it came out in a form which could be gotten through Congress, and the other bankers were there to offer suggestions and help on banking problems. Instead of making a report to Congress or to the American people on the results of the National Monetary Commission's trip to Europe, Senator Aldrich went to Jekyl Island to write a bill which later was passed by Congress and signed by President Woodrow Wilson as the Federal Reserve Act of 1913.

The Jekyl Island group remained at the club for nine days, working steadily to complete their job, for Congress was already complaining that the National Monetary Commission seemed to have no solution ready. Despite the common interests of all present, the work did not proceed without friction. Senator Aldrich considered himself the leader of the group, and, as a dictatorial type, could not help ordering everyone about. Aldrich also felt somewhat out of place as the only member who was not a professional banker. He knew very little about the technical aspects of financial operations, previously having been content to see to it that the country's laws took care of his business for him. Paul Warburg felt that every question demanded a lecture, and he never lost an opportunity to go into a long discourse or to impress the others with the extent of his technical knowledge of banking. This often seemed a waste of time, and drew many barbed remarks from Aldrich, so that it sometimes required all the diplomacy of Henry P. Davison to keep them at their work. Also, Warburg's thick alien accent grated on them all. As the lone outsider in this clique of American aristocrats, he realized the delicacy of his position, but nevertheless quarrelled on any occasion concerning technical problems, which he considered his personal field.

One of the main difficulties in working out a monetary reform plan which could then be presented as the work of the National Monetary Commission was to keep hidden the obvious authorship of the bill. So great was popular resentment against bankers since the Panic of 1907 that no Congressman would dare vote for a bill bearing the Wall Street taint, regardless of who had paid his campaign expenses. The plan which was being worked out at Jekyl Island was a plan for a central bank. There was in American history a long tradition of war against inflicting a central bank on the finances of this country, and there had until 1896 been a continuous struggle against a totalitarian domination of our financial resources. It had begun with Jefferson's fight against Alexander Hamilton's scheme for the First Bank of the

United States It had continued with Andrew Jackson's successful war against Nicholas Biddle's Second Bank of the United States (Biddle had been backed in that fight by James Rothschild of Paris); a fight which was a financial Civil War, and it had resulted in the setting-up of the Independent Sub-Treasury System which supposedly had kept the United States' funds out of the hands of the great bankers. Because our funds were in the Sub-Treasury System, the bankers had precipitated the money panics of 1873, 1893, and 1907, causing widespread suffering throughout the country and arousing the public to demand that Congress enact legislation to prevent the recurrence of artificially inspired money panics. Such monetary reform now seemed inevitable, and it was to head off and control such reform that the National Monetary Commission had been set up with the multi-millionaire Nelson Aldrich at its head. The financiers' inner circle was now gathered at Jekyl Island to write banking legislation which would protect their interests, legislation which would be publicized as a "people's banking bill."

The main problem, so Paul Warburg informed his colleagues, was to avoid the name of "Central Bank", and for that reason he had come upon the designation of "Federal Reserve System." This would allay suspicion in the popular mind that the bill was a central bank plan. However, it would still function as a central bank, fulfilling the three main functions in that tradition, that is, it would be owned by private individuals who would draw profit from ownership of shares, and who could control the nation's issue of money, it would have at its command the nation's entire financial resources, and it would be able to mobilize and mortgage the United States by involving us in major foreign wars.

The next principle consideration was to conceal the fact that the proposed "Federal Reserve System" would be dominated by the operators of the New York money market. The Congressmen from the South and the West particularly could not survive a vote for a Wall Street plan. Farmers and small businessmen in these sections had suffered most from the repeated money panics, and there had been ever since the Revolutionary War considerable amount of popular resentment against Eastern bankers. The private papers and letters of Nicholas Biddle, which were not publicly printed until nearly a century after his death, show that even at that time the Eastern bankers had to take into consideration the feeling against them.

Paul Warburg had already worked out the primary deception which would keep the people from recognizing his plan as a central bank. This was the regional reserve system, an organization of four (later passed as twelve) branch reserve banks located in different sections of the country. No person unacquainted with the details of the nation's credit structure would be likely to realize that the present concentration of most of the nation's debt and money in New York made the operation of a regional reserve system farcical, since the regions would finally be dependent on the amount of money or credits available to them from New York.

Most important of the provisions incorporated in the legislation drafted by the financiers was the selection of the administrators of the Federal Reserve System. Aldrich was the first to point out that the officials should be entirely appointive offices, and that Congress should not have anything whatever to do with them. As an experienced Senator, he knew that any Congressional control over the administration of the System would embarrass the Wall Street interests, because the hick Congressmen would lose no opportunity to investigate irregularities and prove to their constituents that they were fighting the traditional enemies, the Eastern bankers.

Removal of the System from Congressional control and supervision made the entire Federal Reserve proposition unconstitutional from its inception, because the Federal Reserve would be a bank of monetary issue, and Congress is expressly charged in the Constitution with the issuance of money. Article 1, Section 8, Paragraph 5, states that:

CONGRESS SHALL HAVE THE POWER TO COIN MONEY AND REGULATE THE VALUE THEREOF; AND OF FOREIGN COIN. *

Enactment of Warburg's Federal Reserve System meant that the legislative department of our government would lose its sovereignty, and that system of checks and balances of power set up with so great a struggle by Thomas Jefferson in the Constitution would be destroyed. Administrators of the System would control future issue of the nation's money and credit, and would themselves be controlled by the *executive* department of the government. The judicial department, (Supreme Court, etc.) already was controlled by the executive department through the wangle of appointive offices, and now the legislative department would be effectively castrated, making possible a rapid centralization of power behind the White House in Washington.

Four years after the passage of the Federal Reserve Act in 1913, the United States had been involved in the First World War, and was in the grips of an absolute dictatorship of three men, who imprisoned anyone who objected to them. A Presidential candidate of the Socialist Party, Eugene Debs, was sent to Atlanta prison by Woodrow Wilson because Debs failed to applaud the gassing of American youth in Flanders fields. Our heavy industry was under the dictatorship of

*The Supreme Court has held that the delegation of the coinage prerogative to private bankers is Constitutional because Congress thought it "necessary and proper" to do so. "Necessary and proper" says the Court, "means convenient." Of course the most "convenient" method of handling a Constutionally delegated power is to abdicate that power to private interests. (McCulloch vs. Maryland, 4 Wheat 316, 4 L. ed. 579.)

Wall Street gambler Bernard Baruch; food and agriculture were under the dictatorship of a London Exchange gold-manipulator, Herbert Hoover, who had not been in this country as a resident for twenty years prior to his appointment by Woodrow Wilson; and our finances were under the dictatorship of Paul Warburg, chairman of the Federal Reserve Board of Governors, whose first allegiance was to his family banking house of M. M. Warburg Co. of Hamburg. M. M. Warburg was at that time financing the Kaiser's war against us, and Paul Warburg's firm of Kuhn, Loeb Co. had five representatives in the Treasury Department in charge of Liberty Loans, thus financing our war against the Kaiser.

Baruch's partner in the Alaska-Juneau Gold Mining Co., Eugene Meyer, was head of the War Finance Corporation. Eugene Meyer collected commissions on the hundreds of millions of dollars of Liberty bonds which he bought from and sold to himself as head of the War Finance Corporation to Eugene Meyer and Co., 14 Wall St., New York. No wonder he bought control of the enormous chemical trust, the Allied Chemical and Dye Corporation, and became a publisher in Washington, owner of the extremely leftwing Washington Post, the staunch defender of the traitor Alger Hiss.

With power such as this at stake, it is not to be wondered that the Aldrich group traveled a thousand miles in a sealed railroad car to prepare their plans for taking over this country. The writing of the plan, however, was only the first step.

The first serious break in the work of the Jekyl Island group came when Senator Nelson Aldrich declared that he could not let Warburg's proposed designation of "Federal Reserve System" be attached to the bill. His name had already been associated in the public mind with monetary reform, and he argued that it would arouse suspicion if a bill were put before Congress which did not bear his name. Warburg argued in vain that the use of Aldrich's name would certainly condemn the bill as representing the great Wall Street interests, for Aldrich was popularly known for his tariff bills in favor of the tobacco trust and the rubber trust. Aldrich, however, had made up his mind that the legislation must bear the name of Aldrich, and he would not hear any objection to it.

Most of Warburg's suggestions had already been incorporated in the bill, and his colleagues saw in this disagreement a chance to defeat him on at least one point, so that Warburg found himself alone in his opposition to Aldrich. Predicting that the name alone would make their work in securing its passage much harder, if not impossible, he devoted himself to helping them polish up the bill, and, some ten days after they had sneaked out of the city, they returned to New York with a completed financial act which would be presented to Congress under the name of "The Aldrich Plan."

The point which Warburg had most successfully gotten into the plan was the matter of a uniform discount rate, to be imposed on all the banks of the United States by the proposed system. This was the method employed by the big European central banks about which Warburg knew so much. A discount rate imposed by a central bank on the entire nation meant the power to create a money panic not only on the New York money market, as had been the case in the Panics of 1893 and 1907, but also the power to make the money shortage a truly nationwide condition. Consequently, there occurred the Agricultural Depression of 1920-21, and the Great Depression of 1929-31, for both of which, as we shall see, the Federal Reserve System was directly responsible.

In Paul Warburg's Memorandum, quoted in the official biography of Nelson Aldrich, Warburg said:

"The matter of a uniform discount rate was discussed and settled at Jekyl Island."

Although this was Warburg's single reference to Jekyl Island, (a twenty-five hundred page work by him on the Federal Reserve System fails to mention this group in any way), the other members of the "First-Name Club" were not so reticent. In an article in the Saturday Evening Post, in 1935, Vanderlip went into detailed discussion of the Jekyl Island adventure. He said, in introducing the event, that:

"Despite my views about the value to society of greater publicity for the affairs of corporations, there was an occasion, near the end of 1910, when I was as secretive, indeed as furtive, as any conspirator. Since it would have been fatal to Senator Aldrich's plan to have it known that he was calling on anybody from Wall Street to help him in preparing his Bill, precautions were taken that would have delighted the heart of James Stillman (President of the National City Bank during the Spanish-American War)."

Frank Vanderlip further states, in his autobiography, "From Farmboy to Financier":

"Our secret expedition to Jekyl Island was the occasion of the actual conception of what eventually became the Federal Reserve System. The essential points of the Aldrich Plan were all contained in the Federal Reserve Act as it was passed "

In a preface written for a group of Warburg's essays calling for a central bank, Professor E. R. A. Seligman, of the international banking family, head of the Dept. of Economics of Columbia University, said:

"The Federal Reserve Act is the work of Mr. Warburg more than of any other man in the country."

The facts bear out Mr. Seligman's statement.

Chapter Two
SENATOR ALDRICH

With the return of the Jekyl Island group to New York, the financiers now sponsored a nationwide propaganda movement to sell the people on "The Aldrich Plan." All national banks were forced to contribute to a slush fund of five million dollars, and the great universities were used as strongholds of propaganda, abetted by the university presidents and the professors of economics.

Woodrow Wilson, President of Princeton University, was the first prominent educator to speak in favor of the Aldrich Plan, a gesture which immediately brought him the Governorship of New Jersey and later the Presidency of the United States. During the Panic of 1907, Wilson had declared that: "All this trouble could be averted if we appointed a committee of six or seven public-spirited men like J. P. Morgan to handle the affairs of our country." This plea for a financial dictatorship had brought him favorable notice from the bankers, and he had been invited by Frank Vanderlip to a luncheon with James Stillman, then President of the National City Bank. Stillman afterwards remarked to Vanderlip that Wilson was not a great man. Nevertheless, the support of the National City Bank gave Wilson the Presidency of the United States after Wilson promised to enact the Federal Reserve Act.

Much of the bankers' campaign fund was spent under the auspices of an organization called the National Citizens' League, which was not national and might properly have been called an economists' league, since it was made up principally of college teachers who wished to get on in the world. It was headed by J. Laurence Laughlin, the most prominent gold standard economist in the country, and head of the Department of Economics at Rockfeller's University of Chicago. The League soon numbered among its members most of the economists and college presidents in the East and Middle West. The League printed and distributed many abstruse and technical volumes pointing out the need for a central bank and other features of "monetary reform."

The Aldrich Plan was presented to Congress as the result of three years of work, study, and travel of the National Monetary Commission, at an expense of more than three hundred thousand dollars. Actually, only two members of the Commission had anything to do with the plan, Senator Aldrich and A. Piatt Andrew, who was not a member of the commission but a Special Assistant. The other members had a two year joyride around Europe and cheerfully signed everything which Aldrich asked of them.

In 1911, the Aldrich Plan became the official platform of the Republican Party. This was a case of the broom riding the witch, for the Republican Party had ever since the Civil War fought bitterly all efforts at monetary reform up to 1910, and had spent the largest sum of money employed in a Presidential campaign up to that time, in the campaign against William Jennings Bryan in 1896. Bryan was running on a campaign of monetary reform, and was arousing such response that international bankers here and in Europe poured money into a Republican fund and purchased votes by the million. The amount of money spent in that campaign has never been determined with any degree of accuracy, but subsequent Congressional investigations put the figure at from six to eighteen millions of dollars. The same bankers who had given money to fight monetary reform in 1896 were in 1911 giving liberal donations to see that *reform legislation* was enacted

The Republican Party had become identified as the representative of the conservative classes in money matters, and its sudden about-face on this issue caused some suspicion. Monetary reform had until this time been the preserve of the Democratic Party. William Jennings Bryan had very nearly secured the Presidency on a bimetalism platform, although as he remarked to the economist Arthur Kitson, "Free silver is only window-dressing. The real issue is the control of the nation's money and credit." As the candidate of the Democratic Party, Bryan had made his famous "Cross of Gold" speech, in which he enjoined the New York bankers not to crucify the American citizen on a cross of gold. They did not listen to him.

There were still in 1911 many independent and public-minded newspapers, whose editors were not in the pay of bankers and whose mortgages were not subject to foreclosure from New York. These editors saw in the Aldrich Plan its concealed threat to their communities, and began a forceful and vigorous campaign against it. They pointed out, as Paul Warburg had foreseen, that Senator Nelson Aldrich did not represent the common people of this country, or anyone else who had less than a million dollars, and there was plenty of evidence to prove it. Consequently a nationwide opposition sprang up against the Aldrich Plan. The outcry against it created an atmosphere favorable to passing the same plan under the sponsorship of Woodrow Wilson and the Democratic Party as the Federal Reserve Act of 1913.

Louis Brandeis led the fight against the Aldrich Plan in the Harper's Weekly with a series of articles on the Great Money Trust. The period in literary history to be known as the "muckraking" period was then in full swing. Ida Tarbell wrote a series of articles in the American Magazine exposing Senator Aldrich's illegal activities, and a definitive history of Rockefeller's Standard Oil, pointing out that Rockefeller's gigantic expansion would not have been possible without the funds advanced to him by the National City Bank and Kuhn, Loeb Co.

Miss Tarbell graphically described the poverty in which the workers in Aldrich's factories lived, while he grew orchids in hothouses within sight of the slums. Aldrich had secured Senate approval for the great trusts formed in the last decade of the nineteenth century, and he himself was a partner in two of the largest of these corporations, the tobacco trust formed with Duke as its head, and the rubber trust, led by Rockefeller and Guggenheim. The technical aspects of handling these great mergers were perfected by a brilliant young financier named Bernard Baruch, who was just coming into prominence on Wall Street.

Harper's Weekly of May 7, 1910, editorially commented that "Finance and the tariff are reserved by Nelson Aldrich as falling within his sole purview and jurisdiction. Mr. Aldrich is endeavoring to devise, through the National Monetary Commission, a banking and currency law. A great many hundred thousand persons are firmly of the opinion that Mr. Aldrich sums up in his personality the greatest and most sinister menace to the popular welfare of the United States. Ernest Newman recently said 'What the South visits on the Negro in a political way, Aldrich would mete out to the mudsills of the North, if he could devise a safe and practical way to accomplish it'."

The Aldrich Plan was a safe and practical way to accomplish the desires of Aldrich and his class, as was the Federal Reserve Act. Aldrich was a dictator of the banker type which the Communists during the 1920's were to make immortal, the "bloated capitalist" of whom J. P. Morgan became the symbol. The organizers of the trusts had completed most of their work in the previous twenty years, and it was up to them now to secure their gains. This could be done only through control of money and credit, for, under out financial system, ownership of the trusts could not be maintained if somebody came along with more money to buy them. Rubber, steel, heavy industry, railways and public communications were securely in the hands of a few family dynasties, as Ferdinand Lundberg proves in his authoritative work, "American's Sixty Families." The Guggenheims, Seligmans, Schiffs, Warburg, Baruchs, Lehmans, and their satellites, controlled banking and politics. It was certain that the power of these trusts could be attacked in only two ways, by uncontrolled money, and by uncontrolled popular movements which might gain a majority in Congress and force the oligarchy to give way. Thus, the movement for monetary reform coincided with the great reform movement which was designed to corral and emasculate any popular protests against the international elements. Theodore Roosevelt provides an excellent example of this, accepting $500,000 in campaign funds from Schiff and Morgan in 1904 while he was stomping up and down the country bellowing about what he was going to do to the trusts. The trusts survived his term of office.

The Sherman Anti-Trust Act and the Clayton Anti-Trust Act were written by the oligarchy for the oligarchy, to prevent anyone else from breaking into the circle after things had been set up. The result of these "anti-trust" laws has been to render the big corporations secure from popular interference. Thurman Arnold writes in "The Folklore of Capitalism" that:

"The anti-trust laws were the greatest encouragement to the forming of the great corporations."

This was due to the fact that only the giant aggregations of corporate interests could survive the legal entanglements created by government legislation. Small outfits, unable to afford the services of a large legal and administrative staff, were forced to sell out to the trusts. A new profession, that of corporation lawyer, sprang up to devise ways to make the government helpless to regulate the trusts. The Attorney General could bring suit against a corporation to dissolve a "conspiracy in restraint of trade", but, by the time he had secured a court order and begun legal action, the corporation's lawyers would have worked out a new and more foolproof organization. Also, the Attorney General's dissolution of corporations and their subsequent reforming was usually a highly profitable event for the owners. Such a reforming meant that the stocks of the old corporation could be manipulated on Wall Street while action was pending, and the forming of a new organization meant a large issue of stock, most of which would be over-capitalization, so the net result of a Department of Justice action against a corporation often meant the reaping of more millions of dollars for the interests which the Government pretended to attack.

The era of the trust as a dynamic political force had been inaugurated in 1890, when New Jersey passed a law permitting corporations holding incorporations in New Jersey to hold the stock of other corporations, thus permitting the abuse of interlocking directorates, which allow a few men to exercise direct control in many corporations, some of which are supposedly competitors.

The farcical nature of the "reform Presidents" is shown by the record of the first of them, Theodore Roosevelt, who has been nicknamed, perhaps derisively, as the "trust-buster". His friend and financial adviser Colonel Ely Garrison remarks in his memoirs that "Wall Street had no cause for hysteria at the election of Theodore Roosevelt, for any serious student of history knows that the Department of Justice's investigations of Northern Securities and Standard Oil (both Kuhn-Loeb Co. enterprises) were initiated before Roosevelt's election and carried on without his approval."

Theodore Roosevelt also hated the writers who were doing factual research into the activities of the trusts, people like Upton Sinclair, Ida Tarbell, and Frank Norris. It was his private secretary, William Loeb, Jr., who coined the name "muck-raker" for them.

The reform movement, although principally bought out and corrupted, was not without honest spokesman in Congress. Chief among them were Senator La-Follette of Wisconsin in the Senate, and Congressman Charles Augustus Lindbergh of Minnesota in the House of Representatives. Both of these men attacked the Aldrich Plan as a "Wall Street Plan", and through their forceful speeches attracted the people's interest in the doings of the money trust. Their charges eventually resulted in the Pujo Committee Hearings, a Gilbert and Sullivan investigation of the New York bankers at which neither Lindbergh nor LaFollette were invited to officiate or to appear.

Jacob Schiff, senior partner of Kuhn, Loeb Co. had said in a speech before the Chamber of Commerce of New York, shortly before the Panic of 1907:

"Unless we have a central bank with adequate control of credit resources, this country is going to undergo the most severe and far-reaching money panic in its history." The powerful banker's threat soon became a reality. The Panic of 1907, which occurred in a good crop year, when industry was productive and the country enjoyed a general prosperity, aroused public indignation and forced Congress to take a token action against a recurrence by passing the Aldrich-Vreeland Act of 1908. This Act provided for the issuance of currency against securities in case of another money panic. Its provisions were put in use only during the last months of its being, in the early part of 1914, when the sudden withdrawal of large sums of European gold from this country, occasioned by the beginning of the First World War, caused a temporary money stringency. The Federal Reserve Act, although already law, was not yet in operation, and the Aldrich-Vreeland Act was used as the basis for issuing four hundred million dollars to cover a loan due the firm of J. P. Morgan Co. from the Bank of England.

The real purpose of the Aldrich-Vreeland Act was the creation of a National Monetary Commission. Any prospective monetary legislation coming to Congress in the next few years would have to be referred to this body, which effectively prevented the public indignation from manifesting itself in any constructive form. Two years and $300,000 later, under the leadership of Senator Nelson Aldrich, the National Monetary Commission advanced Paul Warburg's Federal Reserve Plan under the name of the Aldrich Plan.

On March 2, 1911, the New York Chamber of Commerce officially adopted a plan of its Special Currency Committee, of which Paul Warburg was then Chairman, for a Central Reserve Bank. This was the same as the Aldrich Plan, except for the distribution of reserves. This plan openly provided for the centralized reserves to be kept in New York, and was immediately branded as the official Wall Street plan, to divert attention from the Wall Street sympathies of the Aldrich Plan.

The campaign for the Aldrich Plan was sincere, in that Aldrich and its supporters in the Republican Party honestly believed that they could win with it and get it enacted into law. More than likely they could have, had they had anyone less notorious than Nelson Aldrich as its head. The Federal Reserve Act, the official platform of Woodrow Wilson and the Democratic Party in 1912, was in all its essentials the same plan for a central bank, and was promoted by the same New York banking interests. It was an alternate stratagem which made it impossible for the bankers to lose. No matter who won the election, they would get their central bank.

The propagandists for the Aldrich Plan carried on their fight without regard for oposition, as evidenced by the following testimony of Andrew Frame, member of the Executive Committee of the American Bankers' Association, testifying before the House Banking and Currency Committee in 1913. Andrew Frame represented a group of Western bankers who were relatively free from the domination of the New York money market, and who were traditionally an opposition group in the American Bankers' Association:

CHAIRMAN CARTER GLASS: "Why didn't the Western bankers make themselves heard when the American Bankers' Association gave its unqualified, and, we are assured, unanimous approval of the scheme proposed by the National Monetary Commission?

ANDREW FRAME: I'm glad you called my attention to that. When that monetary bill was given to the country, it was but a few days previous to the meeting of the American Bankers' Association in New Orleans in 1911. There was not one banker in a hundred who had read that bill. We had twelve addresses in favor of it. General Hamby of Austin, Texas, wrote a letter to President Watts asking for a hearing against the bill. He did not get a very courteous answer. I refused to vote on it, and a great many other bankers did likewise.

MR. BULKLEY: Do you mean that no member of the Association could be heard in opposition to the bill?

ANDREW FRAME: They throttled all argument.

MR. KINDRED: But the report was given out that it was practically unanimous.

ANDREW FRAME: The bill had already been prepared by Senator Aldrich and presented to the executive council of the American Bankers' Association in May, 1911. As a member of that council, I received a copy the day before they acted upon it. When the bill came in at New Orleans, the bankers of the United States had not read it.

MR. KINDRED: Did the presiding officer simply rule out those who wanted to discuss it negatively?

ANDREW FRAME: They would not allow anyone on the program who was not in favor of the bill.

— 19 —

CHAIRMAN GLASS: What significance has the fact that at the next annual meeting of the American Bankers' Association held at Detroit in 1912, the Association did not reiterate its indorsement of the plan of the National Monetary Commission, known as the Aldrich scheme?

ANDREW FRAME: It did not reiterate the indorsement for the simple fact that the backers of the Aldrich Plan knew that the Association would not indorse it. We were ready for them, and they did not bring it up."

Andrew Frame was an honest American banker with no international allegiances, and his testimony received little attention from Carter Glass, who was looking for New York capital to finance his Lynchburg Steel Co. Therefore, Chairman Carter Glass called before the House Committee one of the ten most powerful bankers in America, and one about whom least is known, George Blumenthal, partner of the international banking house of Lazard Freres and brother-in-law of Eugene Meyer, Jr.

Glass effusively welcomed the Blumenthal, saying that "Senator O'Gorman of New York was kind enough to suggest your name to us." O'Gorman figured a year later in preventing a Senate Committee from asking his master, Paul Warburg, any embarrassing questions before appointing Warburg the first Governor of the Federal Reserve Board.

George Blumenthal stated that "Since 1893 (the year of the great Schiff-inspired panic) my firm of Lazard Freres has been foremost in importations and exportations of gold and has thereby come in contact with everybody who had anything to do with it."

Congressman Taylor asked him "Have you a statement there as to the part that you have had in the importation of gold into the United States?" Taylor asked this because the Panic of 1893 is known to economists as a classic example of a money panic caused by gold movements.

"No," replied George Blumenthal, "I have nothing at all on that, because it is not bearing on the question."

Blumenthal was quite right. The question was whether Congress could deliver over the American people, lock, stock, and barrel into the hands of the international financiers, and it was a waste of time to discuss the past crimes of the bankers. They wanted the Federal Reserve Act to provide a government agency which would back them up and help them promote their illegal schemes, and this it has done.

Marriner Eccles, who was Governor of the Federal Reserve Board for the duration of the Roosevelt Regime, 1933-45, recently published his autobiography, "Beckoning Frontiers", an inspiring title of which the book is a complete refutation, for he pleads to close up frontiers and opportunities for individualism. Like his querulous dictator, F. D.

Roosevelt, Marriner Eccles hated freedom. Eccles in this book makes a lengthy presentation of his favorite theory, the compensatory economy.

The compensatory economy provides that when bankers and speculators clean out the people and bring them to their knees, government agencies shall step in and help them up so that they can be fleeced again. This is the function of such agencies as the Securities Exchange Commission, Reconstruction Finance Corporation, and dozens of others. The theory of the compensatory economy supplants all morality in public life, and is responsible for much corruption of officials in Washington. Thus, also, the predilection of the international bankers for putting ignorant provincials into key positions is not an idle fancy, and is perhaps reason for much incessant publicity for democracy. It suits the internationals that public officials should be of the stupidest type, and the guise of democracy effectively controls them.

During the 1920's, the role of the Federal Reserve System and of the Governors of the Federal Reserve Board was nothing more than influential bond salesmanship for such firms as J. & W. Seligman Co. and Kuhn, Loeb Co. of New York. Albert Strauss, partner of J. & W Seligman was a Governor of the Board in the 1920's, and under his capable leadership (he was with Baruch at Paris in 1919), the System made it possible for the New York bankers to sell those foreign bonds by its easy money policies which it followed throughout the 1920's. At no time during these years did the System exercise its delegated responsibility of protecting the American bond-purchaser by warning them that the bonds were being issued on poor or nonexistent collateral.

Edward B. Vreeland, New York subway owner and co-author of the Aldrich-Vreeland Act of 1908, wrote in the August 25, 1910, Independent (owned by Aldrich) that "Under the proposed monetary plan of Senator Aldrich, monoplies will disappear, because they will not be able to make more than four per cent interest, and monopolies cannot continue at such a low rate. Also, this will mark the disappearance of the Government from the banking business."

Just what Mr. Vreeland meant by the Government getting out of the banking business is not clear, unless he meant that in the future the Government would have to pay rent on its own credit, or that the Government's credit would be turned over to private individuals to use for their own profit, in the classic tradition of the central bank. The 145 million dollars worth of stock sold in the Federal Reserve Banks in 1914 was worth, thirty-five years later, more than forty-five billion dollars. It was certainly worth somebody's time and effort to get the Government out of the banking business.

Nation Magazine of January 19, 1911, noted that "The name of

Central Bank is carefully avoided, but the 'Federal Reserve Association', the name given to the proposed central organization, is endowed with the usual powers and responsibilities of a European Central Bank."

After the National Monetary Commission had returned from Europe, it held no official meetings for nearly two years, nor did it ever offer any records or minutes showing *who* had written the Aldrich Plan. Since they had held no meetings, the members of the Commission could hardly claim the Plan as their own. The sole tangible result of the Commission's three hundred thousand dollar expenditure was a library of thirty massive volumes on European banking, none of which directly engaged the financial problems of the United States. Typical of these works is the thousand page history of the Reichsbank, the central bank which controlled money and credit in Germany, and whose principal stockholders were Paul Warburg's family house of M. M. Warburg Co. The Commission's records show that it rarely functioned as a deliberative body. Senator Cummins passed a resolution in Congress ordering the Commission to report on January 8, 1912, and show some constructive result of its three years' work. In the face of this challenge, the National Monetary Commission ceased to exist.

The Aldrich Plan received sound opposition from such writers as Wilbur L. Stonex, who said, in the North American Review of September, 1911:

"Senator Aldrich would take from the people and give to the bankers the absolute control of the people's money. It is apparent that in such a body of bankers there would be no opportunity for the people, or their representatives, to make their wishes known effectively, if their wishes conflicted with those of the banking interests."

It is significant that the North American Review, like many other periodicals which criticized the aims and purposes of the international bankers, has disappeared from the American scene, while other periodicals, like the Nation, have had to change their tune, and favor the international bankers, after Maurice Wertheim of Hallgarten Co. bought control of its stock.

This history of the Federal Reserve Board since 1914 shows that there has never been a method or opportunity for a citizen to protect his interests when the Board has decided upon a change of policy in the interest rate or in their open market operations. Carter Glass fought all efforts to exclude or limit membership of bankers on the Board of Governors of the System, and he was abetted in this effort by Cordell Hull and other powerful Democratic Congressmen in 1913. Glass pointed out that if some of the restrictions of members of the Board were enacted, we would be turning over supervision of our banks to mechanics and farm laborers. Glass' horror at this idea is somewhat strange, since a number of mechanics and farm laborers voted to send him to Congress again and again for thirty years. Also, mechanics in their unions and farm laborers in cooperative associations have done about as good a job in keeping up their credit as have most American bankers.

Congressman Charles A. Lindbergh of Minnesota was one of the most forceful speakers against the Aldrich Plan. He said on the floor of the House of Representatives on December 15, 1911:

"The Aldrich Plan is the Wall Street Plan. It is a broad challenge to the Government by the champion of the Money Trust. It means another panic, if necessary, to intimidate the people. Aldrich, paid by the Government to represent the people, proposes a plan for the trusts instead. It was by a very clever move that the National Monetary Commission was created. In 1907 nature responded most beautifully and gave this country the most bountiful crop it had ever had. Other industries were busy too, and from a natural standpoint all the conditions were right for a most prosperous year. Instead, a panic entailed enormous losses upon us. Wall Street knew the American people were demanding a remedy against the recurrence of such a ridiculously unnatural condition. Most Senators and Representatives fell ito the Wall Street trap and passed the Aldrich-Vreeland Emergency Currency Bill. But the real purpose was to get a monetary commission which would frame a proposition for amendments to our currency and banking laws which would suit the Money Trust. The interests are now busy everywhere educating the people in favor of the Aldrich Plan. It is reported that a large sum of money has been raised for this purpose. Wall Street speculation brought on the Panic of 1907. The depositors' funds were loaned to gamblers and anybody the Money Trust wanted to favor. Then when the depositors wanted their money, the banks did not have it. That made the panic."

Chapter Three
SAMUEL UNTERMYER

The speeches and writings of Senator LaFollette and Congressman Lindbergh had become rallying points for opposition to the Aldrich Plan in 1912. They had also aroused popular feeling against the power of the Money Trust, so that Congress was forced to consider taking action. Congressman Lindbergh said:

"The government prosecutes other trusts, but supports the money trust. I have been waiting patiently for several years for an opportunity to expose the false money standard, and to show that the greatest of all favoritism is that extended by the government to the money trust."

Senator LaFollette made a speech charging that a money trust of fifty men controlled the nation. George F. Baker, partner of J. P. Morgan, on being queried by reporters as to the truth of this sensational accusation, replied that it was absolutely in error. He said that he knew personally that not more than eight men ran this country.

Nation magazine replied editorially to Senator LaFollette that:

"If there is a Money Trust, it will not be practical to establish that it exercises its influence either for good or for bad."

The editors of the Nation apparently had never heard of the Panic of 1907. However, it certainly was not practical to establish the power of the Money Trust. Senator LaFollette remarks in his Memoirs that that speech cost him the Presidency of the United States, just as Woodrow Wilson's speech in favor of the Aldrich Plan had brought him at once to consideration for that office.

Despite the Nation's high-minded detachment, there did seem to be plenty of evidence that the Money Trust exercised its influence for bad. Not only was it despoiling the natural resources of the United States at a rapid rate, but it was not above the most ruthless application of gangster tactics in politics.

Congress finally made a gesture of appeasing popular feeling by appointing a committee to investigate the control of money and credit in the United States. This was the Pujo Committee, which conducted the famous "Money Trust" hearings in 1912, under the leadership of Congressman Arsene Pujo of Louisiana.

The testimony given at these hearings, which dragged on for five months, made four volumes of some six thousand pages. The bankers, month after month, made the train trip down to Washington from New York, testified before the Committee, and returned to New York. The hearings were extremely dull, and those who had expected that much startling information would be turned up at these examinations were disappointed. The bankers solemnly agreed that they were bankers, insisted they operated in the public's interest, and claimed that they were animated by the highest ideals of public service, like the Congressmen. Insofar as the hearings were concerned, this seemed to be true. The bankers were asked few questions which were embarrassing, and nothing was brought out which the public might have been excited by. The newspapers played up the hearings, carrying headlines each day about the Money Trust, but the paragraphs below the headlines had little in them that was interesting.

The nature of the hearings may be better understood if we look at the man who single-handedly carried on the entire investigation, Samuel Untermyer. He was also one of the main contributors to Woodrow Wilson's campaign fund. Untermyer was one of the wealthiest corporation lawyers in New York. He states in his autobiography in "Who's Who in American Jewry" of 1926, that he once received a $775,000 fee for a single legal transaction, the carrying through of the merger of the Utah Copper Company and the Boston Consolidated and Nevada Company, a firm which had at that time a market value of more than a hundred million dollars. A man who could make nearly a million dollars in one operation would not be likely to sincerely attack the wealthy men of his own class.

Neither Lindbergh nor LaFollette, who were responsible for the Money Trust Hearings, were asked to testify or aid in the investigation. A great deal of favorable publicity accrues to politicians associated with such hearings, and the bankers did not wish either of these men to be noticed by the public.

Samuel Untermyer was Special Counsel for the Pujo Committee. The Congressional members of the Committee, including its chairman, Arsene Pujo, seem to have been struck dumb from the moment of the hearings' commencement to their conclusion. An examination of the thousands of pages of minutes reveals that these eleven Congressmen did not ask a dozen questions apiece during the months of investigation. One of these silent servants of the public was James Byrnes, of South Carolina, who later achieved fame as Bernard Baruch's man in charge of the Office of War Mobilization during the Second World War.

Such delicate subjects as the system of interlocking directorates by which a few bankers controlled the nation's finance and heavy industry were not gone into at the Pujo Committee hearings, nor did Samuel Untermyer see fit to dwell upon such items as international gold movements (the cause of money panics), or the international relationships between American bankers and European bankers. The international banking houses of Eugene Meyer, Lazard Freres, J. & W. Seligman, Speyer Brothers, M. M. Warburg, and the Rothschild brothers, did not arouse Mr. Untermyer's curiosity, although it was known that all of these family banking houses either had branches or controlled banking houses in New York City. When Jacob Schiff appeared before the Committee, Mr. Untermyer's adroit questioning allowed Schiff to talk for some minutes without revealing any information about the banking house of Kuhn, Loeb Co., which Senator Robert L. Owen had defined as the representatives of the European Rothschilds in New York.

The aging J. P. Morgan, with only a few more months to live, came before the Committee to justify a half-century of financial piracy. He stated for Mr. Untermyer's edification that "Money is a commodity." Mr. Untermyer did not quarrel with that statement.

J. P. Morgan also declared that, in making a loan, he always considered a man's character before any other factor; even the man's collateral or his ability to repay were not as important. This astonishing observation startled the blase members of the Committee. Here was a banker who began his career by swindling his own government. He sold faulty rifles to the Union Government at a great profit during the Civil War, collecting his money from the Treasury before he paid for his original purchase. He was charged with defrauding the United States. In 1895, he forced President Grover Cleveland to purchase a hundred million dollars worth of gold from the Rothschild brothers after threatening to paralyze the country with another money panic. Mr. Untermyer, however, did not touch upon these incidents in the great man's career.

The farce of the Pujo Committee finally ended. The country was convinced that the New York bankers did have a monopoly on the nation's money and credit. However, the bankers and their subsidized newspapers claimed that the only way to break that monopoly was to enact the banking the currency legislation then before Congress, the bill which was to be passed in the following year as the Federal Reserve Act. The New York monopoly was to be broken by turning over administration of the System to the most powerful of the New York, bankers, Paul Warburg.

Chapter Four
WOODROW WILSON

The Pujo Committee was the last important publicity which the Federal Reserve Act received before being passed in December, 1913. The man who signed it was President Woodrow Wilson, who therefore is thought to be its author. Wilson was elected President of the United States in 1912 on a monetary reform platform. He promised the people of this country that he would give them a money and credit law which would be free from Wall Street influence. At last, he declared, our citizens were going to enjoy the benefits of their own credit, as Thomas Jefferson had intended and provided for in the Constitution.

However good were Woodrow Wilson's intentions, he was limited by the fact that he had been put into office by the biggest Wall Street banking house of them all, Paul Warburg's firm of Kuhn, Loeb Co. His campaign for the Presidency had been entirely financed by Cleveland H. Dodge, of Kuhn, Loeb's National City Bank, Jacob Schiff, senior partner in Kuhn, Loeb Co., Henry Morgenthau, Sr., Bernard Baruch, and Samuel Untermyer. With such a background, as well as his earlier speeches in favor of the Aldrich Plan and his outspoken reverence for J. P. Morgan, the new, Everyman's Woodrow Wilson smacked of ineffectuality, if not downright hypocrisy.

Woodrow Wilson appeared before the people during his campaign with a monetary reform bill written by H. Parker Willis, and officially sponsored by the Democratic Party. A study of this new bill revealed a remarkable similarity to the Aldrich Plan. The more idealistic, and, to the bankers, unrealistic provisions of the bill, providing for others than bankers to administer it, were soon deleted by Carter Glass' House Banking and Currency Committee.

Despite the apparently clean background of the Democratic Party's bill, known as the Federal Reserve Act, it was not favorably received by the country at large, and some newspapers were unkind enough to point out its close kinship to the discredited Aldrich Plan. With such popular opposition already manifesting itself against the people's choice, Woodrow Wilson, Congress did not wish to pass the bill. It required all the political strength of William Jennings Bryan, the dominant power in the Democratic Party, to get Congress to pass the Act.

The Federal Reserve Act, although it was a brother to the Aldrich Plan, was ballyhooed as a people's plan. It promised the American people everything. First of all, it promised to liberate the farmer from his yearly needs for credit to get his crops harvested and send them to market. Heretofore, he had had to go to the bank and mortgage his property for that money. According to the Act's proponents, he could get plenty of credit at the Reserve Bank. This was a bid to get the National Granges to come out in favor of the bill, but they did not rise to the bait. They refused to endorse it, pointing out that its control techniques were not likely to benefit anybody but the bankers, and this was proved when the Federal Reserve System caused the Agricultural Depression of 1920-21.

The next benefit of the Federal Reserve Act, it was claimed, was that it would stabilize the monetary unit and give the dollar a consistent and balanced purchasing power. This was the provision insisted upon by Senator Robert L. Owen, co-author of the Owen-Glass Act, as the Federal Reserve legislation was known in Congress. Glass struck out this stabilization provision. Senator Owen later wrote:

"I was unable to keep this mandatory provision in the bill because of the secret hostilities developed against it, the origin of which at that time I did not fully understand."

The Federal Reserve Act as signed by Woodrow Wilson contained no stabilization mechanism, but it did contain plenty of factors which would make stabilization impossible. Its manipulation of the discount rate to vary the amount of money in circulation, and its open market operations, dumping quantities of Government securities on the New York Exchange or withholding them to create credit expansion or contraction, were the conditions directly responsible for the greatest disaster this country has ever suffered, the Great Depression of 1929-31.

The hostility of the influences behind the Federal Reserve Act towards any kind of monetary stabilization has been expressed in the official publications and statements of the Governors. Marriner Eccles, Chairman of the Board of Governors of the Federal Reserve System, issued a Memorandum March 13, 1939, stating that:

"The Board of Governors of the Federal Reserve System opposes any bill which proposes a stable price level."

Another bit of propaganda for the Federal Reserve Act in 1913 was the claim that it would perform many banking services for the Government without charge. At the Senate OPA Hearings in 1941, Representative Wright Patman inquired of Marriner Eccles:

"Governor Eccles, when did the Federal Reserve System start charging the Government agencies a service charge?"

"I really could not say," replied Mr. Eccles.

"Wasn't it intended when the Federal Reserve Act was passed that the Federal Reserve Bank would render this service without charge—since under the Act the Government would give them the use of the Government's credit free?" asked Mr. Patman.

"I wouldn't think so," answered Mr. Eccles.

To get the Federal Reserve Act made into law, the main lie used was in the flood of speeches and writings poured out in favor of it, was the claim that the nation's money and credit would be released from the domination of a few Wall Street Bankers. The findings of the Pujo Committee were used to frighten the people into submitting to the monetary monster which had them at its mercy. You have got to save yourselves, the spokesmen for the Federal Reserve Act declared, and your saviour is this Federal Reserve System. These spokesmen, led by Representative Carter Glass of Virginia, said that they had devised the perfect way to emasculate the power of Wall Street, namely, the regional reserve system, which would divide the country up into eight or twelve reserve bank districts, depending on whether Mr. Glass or Mr. Warburg made the final choice. Each of these districts would have equal power and equal representation in the administration of the entire reserve system. It was a completely democratic and almost perfect solution. Under the Glass (or Warburg) proposal, Kansas City or Denver would have as much control over the nation's money and credit as New York.

There was only one thing wrong with Glass' system. It ignored the fact that the nation's money market was in New York. Even Marriner Eccles knew that, for he stated at the OPA Hearings that:

"New York is the only money market you have in this country."

This meant that these other reserve banks would have to go to the Federal Reserve Bank of New York whenever they wanted anything, and that they would have to follow the wishes of the Governor of that bank. Consequently, the Federal Reserve System was to fall into the hands of two men during the first fifteen years of its existence, Paul Warburg of Kuhn, Loeb Co., and Benjamin Strong of J. P. Morgan Co.; both of these men were at Jekyl Island when the banking legislation had been written, and both of them knew how to control it. Warburg was on the Board of Governors for four years, and for the ten years after that he dominated the Board by his position as President of the Federal Advisory Council and as President of the American Acceptance Council. Benjamin Strong was Governor of the Federal Reserve Bank of New York from its opening in 1914 until his death in 1928, during a Congressional investigation of the System. That is how Woodrow Wilson freed the nation's money and credit from New York bankers. The regional reserve system could not be anything but a farce. It was designed solely to convince the American people that control of our financial resources was being taken out of Wall Street hands, and, once that was done, the Congressmen could vote for the Federal Reserve Act without fear of reprisal from their constituents.

A Democratic President and a Democratic Congress had been elected in 1912 to get this bill through. Representative Carter Glass of Virginia, Chairman of the House Banking and Currency Committee, gets credit along with Wilson for finally passing the Act, although all that Wilson did was to sign on the dotted line. Woodrow Wilson was regarded generally by the leaders of the Democratic Party as a newcomer and a stuffed shirt. Consequently, he enjoyed little power as President except for the patronage powers he possessed. He could do little towards actually getting Congress to pass the Federal Reserve Act. That job was done by the man who was the Democrat in the minds of the American people, William Jennings Bryan. He acted as Democratic whip to get the Act passed, and he was rewarded by being made the Secretary of State. He later wrote that:

"In my long political career, the one thing I genuinely regret is my part in getting the banking and currency legislation enacted into law."

To still further confuse the American people and to blind them to the real purpose of the Federal Reserve Act, the chief proponents of the Aldrich Plan, Senator Nelson Aldrich and Frank Vanderlip, set up an enthusiastic hue and cry against the bill. They gave interviews to reporters and politicians, anywhere they could find an audience, denouncing the Democratic Party's banking legislation as inimical to bankers and to good government. The old issue of inflation was raised because of the Act's provisions for printing Federal Reserve notes. Both Aldrich and Vanderlip spoke against "fiat money", that is, enough money being put into circulation to assure proper distribution of goods and services among the people. Indeed such was their enthusiasm in speaking against the Federal Reserve Act that they reversed themselves on several matters they had already plugged for in the Aldrich Plan, which brings to mind my grandfather's adage that "Liars should have good memories."

The Nation, on October 23, 1913, points out that:

"Mr. Aldrich himself raised a hue and cry over the issue of government 'fiat money', that is, money issued without gold or bullion back of it, although a bill to do precisely that had been passed in 1908 with his own name as author, and he knew besides, that the 'government' had nothing to do with it, that the Federal Reserve Board would have full charge of the issuing of such moneys."

The Nation was the only public organ, so far as I can find out, which pointed out that the issue of the money of the United States was being turned over to a body of men who were neither elected nor answerable to electors. Later, under Maurice Wertheim, it no longer pointed such criticisms. Aldrich and Vanderlip, in attacking the Federal Reserve Act on these grounds, were throwing up a smoke screen to make people think that the big bankers were afraid of the Act. Paul Warburg discreetly remained silent during the campaign for and against this legislation. He had already arranged, through his private emissary to President Wilson, the ubiquitous Colonel House, that if the Act were passed, Warburg would be chosen one of the first Governors.

Frank Vanderlip, however, threw himself into the comedy with such gusto that Senator Robert L. Owen, chairman of the Senate Banking and Currency Committee, openly accused him of carrying on a campaign of misrepresentation about the bill, as indeed he was. Owen pointed out that Vanderlip, President of the National City Bank of New York, was objecting to just those provisions in the Reserve Plan which he had fought for in the Aldrich Plan. Had Senator Owen known that both plans had originated during the secret expedition to Jekyl Island, he might have been even more vehement in denouncing Mr. Vanderlip. The first public reference to the Jekyl Island adventure, however, was not to appear for three more years, and no one in Washington mentioned it.

Practically all the newspapers and magazines which had any considerable circulation favored the Federal Reserve Act. No economic journal dared to compare the Act with the Aldrich Plan, but such a comparison would show that on most matters, including the introduction of trade acceptances into this country, there was no appreciable difference between the two plans, nor should there have been, since they were written by the same people. The editorial comments in 1913 agreed that if this bill became law, we would enter upon a period of general prosperity such as we had never known. The other extravagant claims for the Federal Reserve Act, its supposed benefits to the farmers, its purpose of stabilizing the integer of account (monetary unit), its functions of performing banking services for the national

Government without charge, and our complete emancipation from Wall Street domination, all have been shown to be lies by the events of the past thirty-five years. The Federal Reserve System has done none of these things, but the biggest lie was that it would end money panics and business depressions. We were to have no more bank failures, no more farms seized by mortgage holders, no more factories closing down or unemployment. The Federal Reserve System could have done a great deal towards ending these things, but it has exerted its influence in the opposite dirction.

The record of the Federal Reserve System proves that it double-crossed the farmers of America at a secret meeting on May 18, 1920, when it raised the rate to 7 percent on agricultural paper and pre-cipitated the Agricultural Depression of 1920-21. It proves that the Board of Governors met with the heads of the great European central banks to make agreements which brought on the Great Depression of 1929-31, after most of our money had been poured into Wall Street because of the easy money policies and credit expansion activities of the System. It proves that the central bank mechanism of the Federal Reserve System involved us in the First World War and the Second World War, and that it is making the Third World War inevitable.

Chapter Five
CARTER GLASS

Despite the growing publicity for the Federal Reserve Act and the influence of William Jennings Bryan on the Democratic Congress, many Senators and Representatives who were familiar with the banking and currency legislation's import were not yet willing to wreck the Constitution and double-cross their constituents by voting for such a bill. The Senate Banking and Currency Committee was ready to write its own version of the Owen-Glass Bill which Representative Carter Glass, Chairman of the House Banking and Currency Committee was ready to send them, but Owen's contribution to the bill, the stabilization of the monetary unit (integer of account) had already been stricken out of the Act. The hearings before the two Committees dragged on for many weeks. Many of the same bankers who had come down from New York to tell all before the Pujo Committee now appeared before Congress to speak in favor of the Federal Reserve Act, a coincidence which the newspapers let pass unnoticed.

Andrew Frame stated before the House Committee that the plan still smacked too much of the government monarchies of Europe, and that it was not in accord with our institutions. This was as close as anybody came to callng the Act unconstitutional, which it was, since it proposed to remove Congress' power of issuing money and credit and turn it over to an appointive body.

— 31 —

Frank Vanderlip declared before the Senate Committee that he now favored the Act, a second reversal of policy in as many months. He had come to the conclusion, he said, that the plan would proceed along democratic lines, since the President would appoint all Board members for ten year terms.

Senator Weeks inquired of him, "Should the Federal Reserve hearings be public, as these hearings are before this Committee?"

"No," replied Mr. Vanderlip, "they are not exactly hearings, they are official meetings." The President of the National City Bank evidently felt that democracy was alright, but that it had to stop somewhere. Carter Glass agreed with him, when he wrote, in "Adventure in Constructive Finance" that:

"The meetings of the Federal Reserve Board are bank board meetings, and neither the public or reporters should be present." Neither Vanderlip nor Glass appears to consider the fact that these "bank board meetings" would be making decisions which would have a more important and more direct impact on the welfare of the American people than the decisions of Congress.

Senator Root also raised the charge of inflation, claiming that under the Federal Reserve Act, note circulation would always expand indefinitely, causing great inflation. The history of the Federal Reserve System refutes this charge. The System has, if anything, kept the note circulation below the amount needed to carry on business and commerce in this country, except during the two World Wars, when it did double and triple the circulation. Even after the Great Depression of 1929-31, when so much of the circulating medium had been withdrawn that the American people had to print their own money on wood and paper, the Federal Reserve System did not increase the amount of notes in circulation.

At the House Committee on Banking and Currency Hearings of 1913, Mr. Paul Warburg testified as follows:

"I am a member of the banking firm of Kuhn, Loeb Co. I came over to this country in 1902, having been born and educated in the banking business in Hamburg, Germany, and studied banking in London and Paris, and have gone all around the world. In the Panic of 1907, the first suggestion I made was 'Let us get a national clearing house'. The Aldrich Plan contains some things which are simply fundamental rules of banking. Your aim in this plan (The Owen-Glass Bill) must be the same—centralizing of reserves, mobilizing commercial credit, and getting an elastic note issue."

Paul Warburg was the most clever of the important New York bankers. In all his writings and speeches and testimonials before Congress, he never made a misstatement. For instance, he did not bother to mention at this appearance that the banking business he had been brought up in in Hamburg, Germany, was his own family banking house of M. M. Warburg Co., a fact which might have been brought up later when he was nominated for the Board of Governors of the Federal Reserve System. Warburg's term "mobilization of credit" was no accident, for the First World War was due to begin in a few months, and the first big job of the System would be to finance the Allies in their war against Germany.

Leslie Shaw, banker from Philadelphia, dissented with most of the other witnesses at these hearings when he testified that:

"Under the Aldrich Plan the bankers are to have local associations and district associations, and when you have a local organization, the centered control is assured. Suppose we have a local association in Indianapolis; can you not name the three men who will dominate that association? And then can you not name the one man who will dominate the three? The same is true in Richmond and everywhere else. When you have hooked the banks together, they can have the biggest political influence of anything in this country, with the exception of the newspapers."

Mr. Shaw did not know that many newspapers were already owned by or mortgaged to, big banks, or that Frank Munsey, agent for J. P. Morgan Co. sometimes bought newspapers to promote a single big stock issue, and sold these periodicals as soon as the stock was unloaded.

The most fiery of the opponents to the Federal Reserve Act was a lawyer from Cleveland, Ohio, named Alfred Crozier, who was the most outspoken critic of the Wall Street banking fraternity. He had written a book in 1912 entitled "U. S. Money vs. Corporation Currency", which attacked the Aldrich-Vreeland Act of 1908 as a Wall Street instrument and pointed out that when our government had to issue money based on privately owned securities, we were no longer a free nation. The Federal Reserve System allowed the issue of notes on the privately owned shares of the Federal Reserve Banks.

Crozier suggested to the Senate Committee that:

"It should prohibit the granting or calling in of loans for the purpose of influencing quotation prices of securities and the contracting of loans or increasing interest rates in concert by the banks to influence public opinion or the action of any legislative body. Within recent months the Secretary of the Treasury of the United States was reported in the open press as charging specifically that there was a conspiracy among certain of the large banking interests to put a contraction upon the currency and to raise interest rates for the sake of making the public force Congress into passing currency legislation desired by those interests. The so-called administration currency bill grants just what Wall Street and the big banks for twenty-five years have been striving for, that is, PRIVATE INSTEAD OF PUBLIC CONTROL OF CURRENCY. It does this as completely as the Aldrich Bill. Both measures rob the government and the people of all effective control over the public's money, and vest in the banks exclusively the dangerous power to make money among the people scarce or plenty. The Aldrich Bill puts this power in one central bank. The Administration Bill puts it in twelve regional central banks, all owned exclusively by the identical private interests that would have owned and operated the Aldrich Bank. President Garfield shortly before his assassination declared that whoever controls the supply of currency would control the business and activities of all the people. Thomas Jefferson warned us a hundred years ago that a private central bank issuing the public currency was a greater menace to the liberties of the people than a standing army."

As the House spokesman for the Democratic Party, Representative Carter Glass took occasion to make public the sorry record of the Republican organization, the National Monetary Commission, in its failure to prepare adequate banking and currency legislation. His House Report in 1913 said:

"Senator MacVeagh fixes the cost of the National Monetary Commission to May 12, 1911, at $207,130. They have since spent another hundred thousand dollars of the taxpayer's money. The work done at such cost cannot be ignored, but, having examined the extensive literature published by the Commission, the Banking and Currency Committee finds little that bears upon the present state of the credit market of the United States. We object to the Aldrich Bill on the following points:

Its entire lack of adequate government or public control of the banking mechanism it sets up.

Its tendency to throw voting control into the hands of the large banks of the system.

The extreme danger of inflation of currency inherent in the scheme.

The insincerity of the bond-refunding plan provided for by the measure, there being a barefaced pretense that this system was to cost the government nothing.

The dangerous monopolistic aspects of the bill.

Our Committee at the outset of its work was met by a well-defined sentiment in favor of a central bank, which was the manifest outgrowth of the work that had been done by the National Monetary Commission."

Representative Glass' denunciation of the Aldrich Bill as a central bank ignored the fact that his own Federal Reserve System would fulfill all the functions of a central bank, that is, its stock would be owned by private stockholders who could use the Government's credit for their own profit, since they would have the privilege of note issue on the Government's credit; it would have control of the nation's money and credit resources, and it would finance the Government by mobilizing credit in time of war. The Federal Reserve System was acknowledged by economists in 1913 to be a bank of issue like the European central banks.

The Federal Reserve Act as Carter Glass presented it was passed by the House virtually intact. It then went to the Senate Committee on Banking and Currency, where such provisions of the Aldrich Bill as were deemed necessary were restored to it. In the Senate debate on the bill, Senator Stone said on December 12, 1913:

"The great banks for years sought to have and control agents in the Treasury to serve their purposes. Let me quote from this World article, 'Just as soon as Mr. McAdoo came to Washington, a woman whom the National City Bank had installed in the Treasury Department to get advance information on the condition of banks, and other matters of interest to the big Wall Street group, was removed. Immediately the Secretary and the Assistant Secretary, John Skelton Williams, were criticized severely by the agents of the Wall Street group.'

'I myself have known more than one occasion when bankers refused credit to men who opposed their political views and purposes. When Senator Aldrich and others were going around the country exploiting this scheme, the big banks of New York and Chicago were engaged in raising a munificent fund to bolster up the Aldrich propaganda. I have been told by bankers of my own state that contributions to this exploitation fund had been demanded of them and that they had contributed because they were afraid of being blacklisted or boycotted. There are bankers of this country who are enemies of the public welfare. In the past, a few great banks have followed policies and projects that have paralyzed the industrial energies of the country to perpetuate their tremendous power over the financial and business industries of America."

The Federal Reserve Act, as altered by the Senate, was finally passed on December 22, 1913, and went to Woodrow Wilson for his signature. Colonel House's connection with Warburg and the Act are revealed in the volume "The Intimate Papers of Colonel House." This Journal contains the following notes:

"Dec. 19, 1912. I talked with Paul Warburg over the telephone, regarding currency reform. I told of my trip to Washington and what I had done there to get it in working order. I told him that the Senate and the Congressmen seemed anxious to do what he desired, TWELVE — the federal reserve conspiracy — L. Rogers and that President-elect Wilson thought straight concerning the issue.

March 13, 1913. Warburg and I had an intimate discussion regarding currency reform.

— 35 —

March 27, 1913. Mr. J. P. Morgan, Jr. and Mr. Denny of his firm came promptly at five. McAdoo came about ten minutes afterward. Morgan had a currency plan already printed. I suggested he have it typewritten, so it would not seem too prearranged, and send it to Wilson and myself today.

Oct. 13, 1913. Paul Warburg was my first caller today. He came to discuss the currency measure. There are many features of the Owen-Glass Bill that he does not approve. I promised to put him in touch with McAdoo and Senator Owen so that he might discuss it with them.

Nov. 17, 1913. Paul Warburg telephoned about his trip to Washington. Later, he and Mr. Jacob Schiff came over for a few minutes. Warburg did most of the talking. He had a new suggestion in regard to grouping the regular reserve banks so as to get the units welded together and in easier touch with the Federal Reserve Board.'' *

Warburg's plan to get the units welded together was merely an indication of his anxiety to get them under as tight a control as possible. House's papers also reveal that it was he who gave Warburg's name to Wilson as candidate for Governor of the first Federal Reserve Board. Wilson approved the choice because of Warburg's interest and experience in currency problems under both Republican and Democratic administrations.

Woodrow Wilson had been piqued by the consistent opposition to the Federal Reserve Act in Congress, and he was haunted by the fear that he would not be able to deliver the goods to his employers. When the bill finally reached him, on December 23, 1913, he refused at first to sign it, because of the provisions for the selection of Class B Directors. Bernard Baruch, relates William L. White in his biography of that great man, a principal contributor to Wilson's campaign fund, hurried over to the White House and told Wilson it did not matter. That could be fixed up later, the main thing was to get the thing signed into law. With this reassurance, Wilson signed the Federal Reserve Act on that December 23, 1913. On that day, the Constitution ceased to be the governing covenant of the American people, and our liberties were handed over to a small group of international bankers.

That same day, Representative Moore of Kansas said, on the floor of the House of Representatives:

*Colonel House was spoken of by Rabbi Wise in his autobiography, "Challenging Years," as the unofficial Secretary of State. It would be more appropriate to call House our unofficial President during the Wilson years, for it was House who was representing us at Versailles, and when Wilson came over, the European politicians laughed at him for his self-importance. They knew who pulled his strings. House also writes in his memoirs that he and Wilson knew that in passing the Federal Reserve Act they had created an instrument more powerful than the Supreme Court. The Federal Reserve Board of Governors is a Supreme Court of Finance, and it forced the Supreme Court to its knees in 1935, when the Justices were made to approve the criminal conspiracy of Roosevelt, Morgenthau, and the international gold dealers to alter the price of gold. If the Justices had disapproved, writes Secretary of the Treasury Morgenthau, "We were ready to rush through an alternate policy."

"The President of the United States now becomes the absolute dictator of all the finances of the country. He appoints a controlling board of seven men, all of whom belong to his political party, even though it is a minority. The Secretary of the Treasury is to rule supreme whenever there is a difference of opinion between himself and the Federal Reserve Board. AND, only one member of the Board is to pass out of office while the President is in office."

The ten year terms of office of the members of the Board, lengthened by the Banking Act of 1935 to FOURTEEN YEARS, meant that these dictators of finance, although not elected by the people, held office longer than any elected official. Now, they hold office longer than three Presidents.

It remained for Congressman Lindbergh to make the final statement on the swindle which had been perpetrated on the American people. Speaking after Representative Moore on that day of December 23, 1913, he said:

"This Act establishes the most gigantic trust on earth. When the President signs this bill, the invisible government by the Monetary Power will be legalized. The people may not know it immediately, but the day of reckoning is only a few years removed. The trusts will soon realize that they have gone too far even for their own good. The people must make a declaration of independence to relieve themselves from the Monetary Power. This they will be able to do by taking control of Congress. Wall Streeters could not cheat us if you Senators and Representatives did not make a humbug of Congress. The division of Congress into political parties is a crime. The main object of the bosses in *both* political parties is to get offices and grant special favors at the people's expense. This is inherently a National Government, and that is why party government is unsuccessful in dealing with economic problems. If we had a people's Congress, there would be stability. The greatest crime of Congress is its currency system. The worst legislative crime of the ages is perpetrated by this banking and currency bill. The caucus and the party bosses have again operated and prevented the people from getting the benefits of their own government."

Lindbergh was overly optimistic in thinking that the trust dictatorship of the United States would last only a few years. The American people have been kept from rising against oppression at home by being sent abroad to fight in two world wars in which we as a people had no immediate political or economic stake. Between wars, two great depressions have kept our people scrambling for their daily bread. They have not had time to object to anything. Lindbergh's theory that party government is unsuccessful in dealing with economic problems could neither be proved or disproved, because party government *has not* dealt with economic problems since the days of Jefferson and

Adams. The architects and contrivers of the economic inequalities and instabilities existing in this country are the leaders and owners of the major political parties. They will not move to improve them.

Chapter Six
PAUL WARBURG

A comparative print of the Federal Reserve Act of 1913 as passed by the House of Representatives and amended by the Senate shows the following impressive changes:

Section 2, Part 2. Provided that the districts shall be apportioned with due regard to the convenience and customary course of business of the community. (The Senate struck out the phrase *'of the community'*.) No Federal Reserve bank shall commence business with a paid up and unimpaired capital less in amount them five million dollars. (The Senate struck out *'paid up and unimpaired'*, and changed the required amount to three million dollars.)

Section 4. Class B directors shall consist of three members who shall be representative of the general public interests of the reserve districts at the time of their election. The Senate struck out *'shall be representative of the general public interests of the reserve districts'*, and added, after the closing word *election*, *'shall be actively engaged in their district in commerce, in agriculture, or in some other industrial pursuit'*.) At a regularly called meeting of the board of directors of each member bank in the reserve district, *the board of directors of such member bank* it shall elect by ballot *one of its own members* a district reserve elector and shall certify his name to the chairman of the board of directors of the Federal Bank of the district. (The Senate struck out all italicized words.) Concerning the election of directors: They shall be fairly representative of the commercial, agricultural, or industrial interests of their respective districts. (This was struck out altogether by the Senate and replaced with): "He shall be a person of tested banking experience."

The Senate also increased the proposed salaries of the Governors of the Federal Reserve System from ten to twelve thousand dollars a year, and struck out, "The Federal Reserve Board shall have the power to remove any director of Class B in any Federal Reserve Bank if it should appear at any time that such director does not fairly represent the commercial, agricultural, or industrial interests in his district."

The following provision was among those struck out by the Senate: "To suspend the officials of Federal Reserve banks for cause, stated in writing with opportunity of hearing, require the removal of said officials for incompetency, dereliction of duty, fraud, or deceit, such removal to be subject to approval by the President of the United States."

The Senate changed this to read as follows:

"To suspend or remove any officer or director of any Federal Reserve bank, the cause of such removal to be forthwith communicated in writing by the Federal Reserve Board to the removed officer or director and to said bank." This changed entirely the conditions under which an official or director might be removed. Under the Senate's clause, we do not know what the conditions are for removal, or the cause. Apparently incompetency, dereliction of duty, fraud, or deceit, do not matter to the Federal Reserve System. Also, the removed officer does not, under this change, have the opportunity of appeal to the President. This removes any possibility that an incoming President, who might be hostile to the incumbent members of the Board, can exercise any control over them. In answer to written inquiry, the Assistant Secretary of the Federal Reserve Board replied that only one officer has been removed "for cause" in thirty-six years, the name and details of the matter being a "private concern" between the individual, the Reserve Bank concerned, and the Federal Reserve Board.

The public really has no right to ask questions of the Board of Governors, for this unique body, although appointed by the President, an elected official, have their salaries paid by' the privately owned member banks. Thus, there is no reason to expect them to place the interests of the public ahead of the interests of the stockholders of the Federal Reserve System, and they have in the past thirty-five years shown unanswering loyalty to their employers.

This review of the changes made by the Senate in the Federal Reserve Act reveals the uncompromising hostility of that body toward any provision of the bill which showed consideration for local representation in the control of money and credit. The very first deletion, of the phrase "of the community", typifies the attitude of the Senate toward the interests of the American people, which was sworn to represent those interests.

In the past twenty years, occasional disagreement has arisen between the principals of this drama as to which of them was most responsible for riveting this yoke on the necks of the American people. Paul Warburg never came out and said that he wrote the bill, or did he ever mention Jekyl Island, except in a privately published memorandum. However, he did collect his writings in a twenty-five hundred page volume on the Federal Reserve System, which proved conclusively that it all originated in his banker's brain.

The late Senator Carter Glass of Virginia, in his book written on the subject, "Adventure in Constructive Finance", took credit for writing the Act. This caused Samuel Untermyer, one of the real authors, to write a letter to his son commenting on this claim, saying that Glass must be senile to put such a bald misstatement into print. Glass later listed himself in Who's Who in America merely as the patron and sponsor of the bill for the House of Representatives. H. Parker Willis, Paul Warburg, and Samuel Untermyer were the principal writers of the administration bill which the Democratic Party presented to Congress. All the important provisions of this bill stem directly from Paul Warburg's work at Jekyl Island. When he was asked by Carter Barron whether he approved of the bill as it was finally passed, Warburg remarked, "Well, it hasn't got quite everything we want, but the lack can be adjusted later by administrative processes." To make certain that those "administrative processes" would begin as he wished, he had Colonel House appoint him as the first Chairman of the Board of Governors of the Federal Reserve System.

Woodrow Wilson and Carter Glass are given full credit for the Act by contemporary historians, but of all the politicians concerned, Wilson had least to do with the fight over the Act in Congress. George Creel, veteran Washington correspondent, wrote in the Harper's Weekly of June 26, 1915, that:

"As far as the Democratic Party was concerned, Woodrow Wilson was without influence, save for the patronage he possessed. It was Bryan who whipped Congress into line on the tariff bill, on the Panama Canal tolls repeal, and on the currency bill. Mr. Bryan later wrote, 'That is the one thing in my public career that I regret—my work to secure the enactment of the Federal Reserve Law."

When Wilson signed the Federal Reserve Act on December 23, 1913, he fulfilled the pledge he made to the men who had financed his campaign. Cleveland H. Dodge of Kuhn, Loeb's National City Bank, Jacob Schiff of Kuhn, Loeb Co., Bernard Baruch, the brilliant young speculator and organizer of the tobacco and rubber trusts, Samuel Untermyer, the multi-millionaire corporation lawyer, and Henry Morgenthau, Sr., the Harlem real estate speculator, never made a better investment than when they purchased the White House for Woodrow Wilson. The money and credit resources of the United States were now in the complete control of the bankers' alliance between J. P. Morgan's First National Bank group and Kuhn, Loeb's National City Bank interests, whose principal loyalties were to the international banking interests then quartered in London, and which moved to New York during the First World War.

Senator Nelson Aldrich now decided that he had not been really opposed to the Federal Reserve Act after all. In a magazine which he owned, entitled, appropriately enough, the Independent, he wrote:

"Before the passage of this Act, the New York bankers could only dominate the reserves of New York. Now we are able to dominate the bank reserves of the entire country."

An interesting observation on the origins and purpose of the Federal Reserve Act was made by Colonel Ely Garrison, friend and financial adviser to Presidents Theodore Roosevelt and Woodrow

Wilson. In his autobiographical book, "Roosevelt, Wilson, and the Federal Reserve Law", Garrison wrote:

"Paul Warburg is the man who got the Federal Reserve Act together after the Aldrich Plan aroused such nationwide resentment and opposition. The mastermind of both plans was Baron Alfred Rothschild of London."

Colonel Garrison moved in the inner circles of high finance, being an international agent of Brown Brothers, bankers, of New York.

The most important revelation of the intent of the Federal Reserve Act of 1913 occurs in a brief observation in the Nation on December 25, 1913.

"THE NEW YORK STOCK MARKET BEGAN TO RISE STEADILY UPON NEWS THAT THE SENATE WAS READY TO PASS THE FEDERAL RESERVE ACT."

This item would seem to contradict the claims of the admirers of Woodrow Wilson and Carter Glass that the Federal Reserve Act was a monetary reform bill. Had there been any possibility that the Act would carry out any monetary reforms whatsoever, that is, that it would reduce the centralization of the nation's money and credit in New York, the Stock Exchange might have had as disastrous a day as the famous Black Thursday of 1929. The New York Stock Exchange is the most accurate barometer of the true meaning of any financial legislation passed in Washington. Whenever legislation is passed which restricts the dictatorship of The New York bankers, as on the occasion of the Glass-Steagall Act of 1933, which provided that banking houses could not be engaged simultaneously in investment banking and deposit banking, the stock market has a bad day. Whenever legislation as favorable to the big financiers as the Federal Reserve Act is passed, prices of stocks rise rapidly.

E. W. Kemmerer, famous economist of Princeton, states in his "A B C of the Federal Reserve System" that:

"The federal reserve banks are essentially bankers' banks." This would indicate that other claims for the bill are false.

Benjamin Strong, in an introduction to the same volume, says:

"The managers of the new federal reserve banks soon found that the welcome accorded to them by the banks of the country was, to say the least, cool. Both bankers and business men were regrettably ignorant of what the Act really meant." The propaganda for the Act had been so devious that, once the bankers had the Act passed, they could not get the country to understand how it should work.

S. E. Harris gives a fair estimate of the Federal Reserve Act in a critique published in the Quarterly Journal of Economics in 1931:

"Glass and his colleagues on the House Banking and Currency Committee in 1913 provided for a regional system in which control occupied a relatively unimportant place, but a measure of control was introduced through acceptance by Glass of suggestions in the

Aldrich Plan, and through the influence of Bryan and the Senate. In the Federal Reserve Act of 1913 there remained but a small proportion of the provisions which had been in the early drafts of the Glass Bill. Warburg during the entire period excercised an important influence on the progress of the legislation through his work on the Aldrich Bill, and through his direct contact with the Senate Banking and Currency Committee."

Further corroboration of Mr. Warburg's work is given by J. Laurence Laughlin in his definitive volume, "The Federal Reserve Act, Its Origins and Purposes":

"Mr. Paul Warburg, of Kuhn, Loeb Co., offered in March 1910 a fairly well-thought out plan to be known as the United Reserve Bank of the United States. This was published in the New York Times of March 24, 1910. The group interested in the purposes of the National Monetary Commission met secretly at Jekyl Island for about two weeks in December, 1910, and concentrated on the preparation of a bill to be presented to Congress by the National Monetary Commission. The men who were present at Jekyl Island were Senator Aldrich, H. P. Davison of J. P. Morgan Co., Paul Warburg of Kuhn, Loeb Co., Frank Vanderlip of the National City Bank, and Charles D. Norton of the First National Bank. No doubt the ablest banking mind in the group was that of Mr. Warburg, who had a European banking training. Senator Aldrich had no special training in banking."

The Federal Reserve Act soon disappointed many people who had believed in it. W. H. Allen wrote in Moody's Magazine in 1916, that:

"The purpose of the Federal Reserve Act was to prevent concentration of money in the New York banks, by making it profitable for country bankers to use their funds at home, but the movement of currency shows that the New York banks gained from the interior in every month except December 1915 since the Act went into effect. The stabilizing of rates has taken place in New York alone. In other parts, high rates continue. The Act, which was to deprive Wall Street of its funds for speculation, has really given the bulls and the bears such a supply as they have never had before. The truth is, that, far from having clogged the channel to Wall Street, as Mr. Glass so confidently boasted, it actually has widened the old channels and opened up two new ones. The first of these leads directly to Washington and gives Wall Street a string on all the surplus cash in the United States Treasury. Besides, in the power to issue banknote currency, it furnishes an inexhaustible supply of credit money; the second channel leads to the great central banks of Europe, whereby, through the sale of acceptances, virtually guaranteed by the United States Government, Wall Street is granted immunity from those foreign demands for gold which have precipitated every great crisis in our history."

Chapter Seven
MORE PAUL WARBURG

When the Federal Reserve Banks were set up and began operations on November 16, 1914, their total assets were listed at $143,-000,000. On December 23, 1949, testimony before the House Banking and Currency Committee showed that the Federal Reserve Banks listed assets in excess of forty-five billion dollars ($45,000,000,000), or, the equivalent of the entire national budget for any year since 1945. The men who bought stock in those Federal Reserve Banks in 1914 made one of the most fortuitous investments in financial history. The percentage of profit is so enormous that it would take an economist from Rockefeller's University of Chicago to compute it.

The men whom President Woodrow Wilson chose to make up the first Federal Reserve Board of Governors were men representing that millionaire class on whom he inclined to fawn. As President of Princeton University, Wilson had developed a fanatical reverence for the "captains of industry" and "monarchs of finance" who built new buildings and endowed chairs of early Andrassian endocrinology for his college. His nomination for the Presidency by the Democratic Party, which had traditionally represented "the common people" against the "vested interests" marked the death of that organization as spokesman for the American people.

According to Wilson himself, he was allowed to choose only one man for the Federal Reserve Board. The others were chosen by the New York bankers. Wilson's choice was Thomas D. Jones of Chicago, director of many large corporations, and a trustee of Princeton University. The other members were Adolph C. Miller, economist from Rockefeller's University of Chicago and Morgan's Harvard University, also Assistant Secretary of the Interior. Miller was one of those independently wealthy men who devoted his life to public service, later a neighbor and close friend of the mining promoter Herbert Hoover.

Charles S. Hamlin, for eight years previously an Assistant Secretary of the Treasury.

F. A. Delano, of the Roosevelt family, a railroad engineer who took over a number of railroads for Kuhn, Loeb Co. which had gone into receivership.

W. P. G. Harding, President of the First National Bank of Atlanta.

Paul Warburg, of Kuhn, Loeb Co.

Secretary of the Treasury William McAdoo, President of the Hudson Manhattan Railroad, a Kuhn, Loeb Co. enterprise.

Comptroller of the Currency John Skelton Williams.

Both Williams and McAdoo were to come even more directly under the control of Kuhn, Loeb Co. during the First World War, when they were appointed by Wilson as Director and Assistant Director of the United States Railroad Administration in 1917-18. Kuhn, Loeb Co. at that time owned or controlled nearly all of the large railroads of the United States.

Paul Warburg, according to "The Intimate Papers of Colonel House", was appointed because "The President accepted the suggestion (House's suggestion) of Paul Warburg of New York because of his interest and experience in currency problems under both Republican and Democratic Administrations."

The brief history of Kuhn, Loeb Co. is given in this quote from Newsweek of February 1, 1936:

"Abraham Kuhn and Solomon Loeb were general merchandise merchants in Lafayette, Indiana in 1850. As usual in newly settled rgeions, most transactions were on credit. They soon found out that they were bankers. Gradually forgetting all about merchandise, they moved West. In Cincinnati, they got considerable help from the Civil War. In 1867, they established Kuhn, Loeb Co., bankers, in New York City, and took in a young German immigrant, Jacob Schiff, as partner. Young Schiff had important financial connections in Europe. After ten years, Jacob Schiff was head of Kuhn, Loeb, Kuhn having having died, and Loeb retired. Under Schiff's guidance, the house brought European capital into contact with American industry, which was then badly in need of it. The Union Pacific had used up a lot of funds, and the railroad failed to earn a return. The Panic of 1893 added the finishing touch. That failure was a boon to Kuhn, Loeb. By financing E. H. Harriman's plans for a new Union Pacific, the firm set itself up as the chief financial backer of American railways."

Jacob Schiff's 'important financial connections in Europe' were the Rothschild Brothers, and their principal German agents, the family Warburg. Paul Emden writes, in "The Money Power of Europe":

"The Warburgs reached their outstanding eminence during the last twenty years of the past century, simultaneously with the growth of Kuhn, Loeb Co. in New York, with whom they stood in a personal union and family relationship. Paul Warburg with magnificent success carried through in 1913 the reorganization of the American banking system at which he had with Senator Aldrich been working since 1911, and thus most thoroughly consolidated the currency and finances of the United States."

By consolidation, Paul Emden meant bringing under control, or, to use Warburg's favorite term, "mobilization of credit." Schiff had been sent over here to set up new representation in America for the Rothschild family. August Belmont had been for some years the only American agent for the Rothschilds, and they wanted a new outlet. The firm of Kuhn, Loeb was ideal for their purpose, and Schiff bought it. It has never been Kuhn, Loeb since, but it has been mostly

Schiff, Warburg, Hanauer, and Strauss. Schiff was given all the capital he needed to buy up American railroads for the Rothschild family. With the death of August Belmont, the Belmont firm went into a decline, the younger son Perry Belmont, going into politics. He later became Chairman of the House Committee on Foreign Affairs. His political work did not entirely divorce him from financial interests, however, and one foreign affair netted him a commission of two million dollars, his payment for negotiating the gold bond deal in 1895 with President Grover Cleveland and the Rothschild family.

Paul Warburg and his brother Felix came to this country in 1902 to get a central bank plan passed. Paul Warburg devoted nearly all his time to agitating for his own brand of banking reform, writing and lecturing at great length on the obsolete credit structure of Wall Street and publishing several volumes of arguments which proved that we needed a central bank mechanism such as the Reichsbank, the Bank of France, and the Bank of England. He particularly attacked the Sub-Treasury System which Andrew Jackson had set up in 1836 to handle our country's funds after he had crushed the Second Bank of the United States in a financial Civil War. It was Warburg's contention that the Independent Sub-Treasury System did not get money to panic centers in time when there was a money shortage, and this was true. During the Panic of 1893, when New York bankers suddenly shipped a hundred million dollars in gold out of this country to Canada and England, the ensuing money panic caused Congress to repeal the Sherman Silver Act and put the nation back on the gold standard. This Panic also drove the price of Union Pacific stock down from 69 1-2 to 47, enabling Jacob Schiff to secure control of the railroad at a great savings for the Rothschild family. When these two goals had been accomplished, the hundred million dollars in gold came back from Canada and England, and the Panic was over. Our national government was helpless against the international gold dealers. Warburg claimed that a central bank with a reserve system would end such panics. The history of the country since 1913 does not agree with him.

Despite the fact that Paul Warburg did not seem to pay attention to the business of his firm of Kuhn, Loeb Co., the other partners evidently thought enough of him to pay him five hundred thousand dollars a year while he was writing and speaking in favor of monetary reform. Before the First World War, this was an extremely large salary. After Warburg carried through this banking reform, he was reluctant to let it be set up without taking a still more active part in it, and so he resigned his five hundred thousand dollar a year job to take the twelve thousand dollar a year position offered him by Woodrow Wilson. Despite such a desertion of his partners, they were considerate enough to let him return at his old salary when he suddenly resigned from the Board of Governors, in May, 1918. Someone had commented upon the fact that his brother was head of the German Secret Service, while his family banking house, M. M. Warburg Company of Hamburg and Amsterdam, was playing its role of chief financial agent for the Kaiser. We had been at war for more than a year before Paul Warburg thought he should resign.

"Who's who in American Jewry" lists Paul Warburg as a partner or director in the following companies and corporations:

Western Union, Westinghouse, Wells Fargo, Union Pacific Railroad, Baltimore and Ohio Railroad, Kuhn, Loeb Co., American I. G. Chemical Co. (I. G. Farben), Agfa Ansco Corp., National Railways of Mexico, International Acceptance Bank (chairman of the board), Westinghouse Acceptance Co., Warburg Co. of Amsterdam, and numerous other banks, railways, and corporations.

Despite Warburg's tremendous influence, there was open opposition in the United States Senate to his appointment as Governor of the Federal Reserve System. He was asked to appear before a Senate Subcommittee in June of 1914 and answer some questions about his activities in connection with getting the Act through Congress, but he refused to appear.

The Nation, on July 23, 1914, said:

"Mr. Warburg finally had a conference with Senator O'Gorman and agreed to meet the members of the Senate Subcommittee informally, with a view to coming to an understanding, and to giving them any reasonable information that they might desire. The opinion in Washington is that Mr. Warburg's confirmation is assured." "Reasonable information", of course, would not include any information about Mr. Warburg's connections with Europe. Above all, he knew the dangers of appearing and being questioned before a formal committee where the hearings might be published later on. He therefore refused to appear at any formal meetings, and forced the Sub-committee to meet with him informally. The minutes of this meeting were not publicized.

Senator Robert L. Owen charged that Warburg was the American representative of the European Rothschilds, but this did not prevent the Senate from confirming him.

The newspapers took very little notice of the disagreements over Warburg's appointment. A great hue and cry had been set up over Wilson's appointment of Thomas D. Jones of Chicago, apparently because Mr. Jones *was at that time under indictment by the Attorney General of the United States.*

The dictatorial nature of Woodrow Wilson always manifested itself whenever there was public criticism of his actions, and he was angered by the unfavorable comments on Warburg and Jones. In attempting to defend his appointment of these men, Wilson made one of the most ridiculous statements ever spoken by a President of the United States. He told reporters that:

"THE MAJORITY OF THE MEN CONNECTED WITH WHAT WE HAVE COME TO CALL 'BIG BUSINESS' ARE HONEST, INCORRUPTIBLE, AND PATRIOTIC."

Wilson's ignorance of the true history of the men whom he admired so much is amazing and inexcusable in a man in charge of the nation's welfare. He did not know that J. P. Morgan had swindled his own government in time of war, or that Otto Kahn and E. H. Harriman had been prosecuted several times for thier illegal activities in their war to obtain control of the Union Pacific Railroad for Kuhn, Loeb Company. There is ample documentation available to prove the criminal history of the international bankers who were Wilson's masters and gods.

Woodrow Wilson further committed himself as an ignorant provincial when, in response to the projected hearings before the Senate Banking and Currency Committee on the fitness of Thomas D. Jones to be a member of the Federal Reserve Board of Governors, he wrote the following letter to Senator Robert L. Owen, chairman of that Committee:

White House,
June 18, 1914.
Dear Senator Owen:
    Mr. Jones has always stood for the rights of the people against the rights of privilege. His connection with the Harvester Company was a public service, not a private interest. He is the one man of the whole number who was in a peculiar sense my personal choice.

Sincerely,

Woodrow Wilson

It is indicative of Woodrow Wilson's character and allegiances that the one man who was in a peculiar sense his personal choice for a high Government office should have been a man under indictment for his participation in a criminal conspiracy against the people of the United States. He was to continue choosing such men to run this country after he led us into the First World War.

The sheer idiocy of Wilson's statements in the foregoing letter are proved by the Senate Hearings on Thomas D. Jones, a document first printed in secrecy which establishes that Jones' "public service" as a director of the International Harvester Company consisted solely of voting himself and his partners a twenty million dollar dividend. In his fight for "the rights of the people against the rights of privilege", it never occurred to Mr. Jones to make any effort to dissolve the International Harvester Company's criminal combination in restraint of trade, even after the Company was indicted by the Department of Justice, and thirty-nine years later, it exists as the identical monopoly which the Attorney General attacked in 1913.

The following official Government documents give the lie to Woodrow Wilson's recommendation of Thomas D. Jones:

Executive Report No. 1, 63rd Congress, 2nd Session.

NOMINATION OF THOMAS D. JONES. JULY 25, 1914.

Ordered to be printed in confidence.

July 21, 1914. Injunction of Secrecy Removed.

Mr. Hitchcock's Adverse Report on Nomination of Thomas D. Jones to be a Member of the Federal Reserve Board, from the House Committee on Banking and Currency. Sen. Document 552.

"The Committee on Banking and Currency herewith reports to the Senate on the appointment of Mr. Thomas D. Jones, nominated to be a member of the Federal Reserve Board, and recommends that the Senate decline to advise and consent to the same. This recommendation is based on the fact that Mr. Jones is an active director in the Harvester Trust and one of the founders and directors of the Zinc Trust. The first has been judicially declared to be an unlawful conspiracy in several States and is now being prosecuted by the United States. The latter has established a practical monopoly in oxide of zinc, has raised the price to consumers, and on a total capital of ten million dollars is making an unconscionable profit of five million dollars a year. The Harvester Trust was organized in 1902 under the name of the International Harvester Company, with a total capital of a hundred twenty million dollars. It was formed and financed by J. P. Morgan Company, who received four million dollars worth of stock; ten million dollars worth of stock was sold for cash to the Rockefellers and others through the J. P. Morgan Company."

Wilson's selling of his sacred trust to the financial oligarchy is absolutely documented by such reports. The Senate Hearings on Nomination of Thomas D. Jones bear out Wilson's betrayal of the American people.

Senate Hearings on Nomination of Thomas D. Jones. July 6, 1914:

SENATOR SHAFROTH: After the hearing is through, we can then determine whether or not it should be made public.

SENATOR CRAWFORD: Primarily the notes taken here are for our use and service, and when we get through with them, they are for the use of the Senate. That is where they belong, rather than to the public.

(This is an instance of our elected representatives carrying out their sworn obligations to the people of the United States. The Hearings were not then made available to the newspapers or to the public.)

SENATOR REED: Now, Mr. Jones, what did you do, if anything, toward endeavoring to secure a dissolution of this monolpoly in restraint of trade here in the United States, which the Attorney General was charging and complaining was a monopoly?

— 48 —

MR. JONES: I cannot claim, Senator, that I advanced any proposal.

SENATOR REED: Did you ever make any motion to the Board of Directors to split it up and make it conform to the requirements of the Attorney General?

MR. JONES: I did not.

SENATOR REED: Did you ever vote for such a proposition?

MR. JONES: Such a proposition never came to a vote.

SENATOR REED: You knew the International Harvester Company was a combination in restraint of trade?

MR. JONES: Yes, sir.

SENATOR REED: You accorded with the general practices of the Company while you were in it?

MR. JONES: I knew of no practices in the Company after I became a director that I thought in any way in contravention of law or good morals.

SENATOR NELSON: What are the profits of the New Jersey Zinc Company, in which you are also a director?

MR. JONES: They paid dividends of about five million dollars last year and four million dollars the year before.

SENATOR HITCHCOCK: What was the capital?

MR. JONES: Ten million dollars.

SENATOR NELSON: It is a profitable thing?

MR. JONES: The dividends were not, strictly speaking, profits.

SENATOR REED: Were you present at the meeting of the International Harvester Company at which the stock dividend of twenty million dollars was declared?

MR. JONES: I was.

SENATOR REED: Did you favor that or oppose it?

MR. JONES: I favored it "

These hearings refute Woodrow Wilson's absurd claims that Thomas D. Jones was a public servant. The Senators hesitated to recommend Jones for the Board of Governors, and deliberated several more weeks. The nation's newspapers shouted Shame at Senator Reed for slandering such a fine man as Mr. Jones.

Woodrow Wilson said: "There is no reason to believe that that unfavorable report represents the attitude of the Senate itself." After several weeks, Thomas D. Jones withdrew his name, and the country had to do without his services.

Chapter Eight
BERNARD BARUCH

When the Federal Reserve Banks were opened for business on the 16th of November, 1914, Paul Warburg said:

"This date may be considered as the Fourth of July in the economic history of the United States."

It was certainly the date when everything which the Fourth of July had stood for, freedom at home and indpendence from foreign influences, was ended.

The magazines and newspapers of this country hailed the opening as a genuine monetary reform. From the facts at hand at that time, it is difficult to see how even the extraordinarily gullible American public swallowed such a lie. The presence of Paul Warburg on the Board of Governors was enough to convince anyone that Wall Street was in charge, and the further appointment of a Federal Advisory Council, a group of bankers to *assist* the Federal Reserve Board in its work, indicated New York influence, for its first members numbered Winthrop Aldrich and J. P. Morgan, Jr.

The Federal Reserve Board is the best illustration of the fact that this country is governed principally by non-elective officials. The career of Henry L. Stimson also bears this out. Law partner of Winthrop and Stimson, he was the close associate of Bronson Winthrop, director of many corporations owned by Kuhn, Loeb Co. Stimson was overwhelmingly defeated when he ran as the Republican candidate for Governor of New York in 1910. He never again tried for elective office, but he was subsequently Secretary of War in President Taft's cabinet, briefly a Colonel in the First World War, until he resigned suddenly on August 8, 1918, the facts of the case being sealed in a confidential file, Governor-General of the Philippines, Secretary of State in Hoover's Cabinet, and Secretary of War in President Roosevelt's Cabinet during the Second World War.

The choosing of the Federal Reserve Districts in 1914 had been the occasion of much good-humored provincialism, with every city of any consequence demanding to be the site of one of the twelve Federal Reserve Banks. After considerable lobbying, the Federal Reserve Bank Organization Committee, consisting of the Secretary of the Treasury, the Secretary of Agriculture, and the Comptroller of the Currency, selected the twelve districts, which were New York, Boston, Philadelphia, Cleveland, Chicago, St. Louis, Richmond, Atlanta, Dallas, Minneapolis, Kansas City, and San Francisco. The great areas of the Western States were left without representation, as was Michigan and Wisconsin, the area which had backed LaFollette in his fight against the Money Trust. The West was also left without representation because of the opposition to the Federal Reserve Act by Andrew Frame and a group of Western bankers in the American Bankers' Association.

In Dallas and Kansas City, the influence of the new Reserve Banks was seriously challenged by the powerful Dallas Joint Land and Stock Bank and the Kansas City Joint Land and Stock Bank. A feud began between the Reserve Banks and these banks, independent institutions which represented the financial needs of the farmers and cattlemen, which was to end melodramatically in 1928, when

United States Marshals, with drawn guns, were to enter the Joint Stock Banks and take them over, obeying the orders of Assistant Secretary of the Treasury Dewey and Eugene Meyer, Jr. The resulting publicity caused the ruin of these banks, and left the Reserve Banks in Dallas and Kansas City at last in complete control of money and credit in their respective districts. These local fights, however, were not too important, as Ferdinand Lundberg was to point out in "America's Sixty Families", when he noted that:

"In practice, the Federal Reserve Bank of New York became the fountainhead of the system of twelve regional banks, for New York was the money market of the nation. The other eleven banks were so many expensive mausoleums erected to salve the local pride and quell the Jacksonian fears of the hinterland." Lundberg goes on to comment that:

"Benjamin Strong, one of the original Jekyl Island group, and President of the Bankers Trust Co. of New York (Morgan) was selected as the first Governor of the New York Federal Reserve Bank. An adept in high finance, Strong for many years manipulated the country's monetary system at the discretion of directors representing the leading New York banks. Under Strong, the Reserve System was brought into interlocking relations with the Bank of England and the Bank of France. Benjamin Strong held his position of Governor of the Federal Reserve Bank of New York until his sudden death in 1928, during a Congressional investigation of the secret meetings between Reserve Governors and heads of European central banks which brought on the Great Depression of 1929-31."

Paul Warburg had always agreed with the idea of a' regional system, but he saw no reason to waste money setting up twelve banks, when four would do just as well. He finally tried to settle for eight, but Carter Glass convinced him that they could never get the Act through Congress with fewer banks than twelve, which occasioned Warburg's remark at that time, that the Act did not contain everything that they wanted, but that could be corrected by administrative processes.

On October 29, 1915, a committee composed of Paul Warburg, Delano, and Hamlin tried to enact Warburg's first administrative process as Governor of the Federal Reserve System. This was an attempt to disestablish the Dallas and Kansas City branches on account of the competition they were receiving in those cities from the Joint Land and Stock banks. The Board's general counsel advised Warburg that the Federal Reserve Act did not give the Board of Governors power to abolish or reduce any districts, but Warburg immediately hired a special counsel to deliver a favorable opinion (Bulletin 1916, pp. 20, 25; 1915, p. 396). Finally, on November 22, 1915, the Attorney General of the United States, to whom the question had been submitted, held that the Board was without power to abolish any of the then existing districts, rendering Warburg his only defeat as dictator of the Federal Reserve System. He had been particularly anxious to get the Dallas and Kansas City Reserve Banks either in control of their districts, or else do away with them, for he was engaged in setting up the System to perform the most important function of a central bank, mobilizing a nation's money and credit to finance a major war.

Bernard Baruch stated before the Nye Committee on September 13, 1937, that:

"All wars are economic in their origin."

Mr. Baruch's own economic interests have made him a dominant power in this country in both World Wars, in the First, when he put Woodrow Wilson in the White House, and in the Second, when he ordered Congress to accept his rationing system, price control system, and labor control system in a series of lectures to the Nye Committee, which laid down the principles of the Roosevelt dictatorship from 1940 to 1945.

The economic aspects of the First World War have been gone into at great length and small profit by many writers who are scholastically qualified to deal with that subject, but the quantity of special grants and fellowships to such people has elicited little more information than Mr. Baruch's statement. Particularly surprising, however, is the complete silence concerning the direct responsibility of the Federal Reserve System for financing Europe in the First World War.

Before 1914, and the setting up of the Federal Reserve System, the United States was a debtor nation, that is, we borrowed a great deal of money from abroad, and we made few international loans, mainly because our money and credit was not mobilized into a central bank. The New York money market was capable of financing industrial enterprises abroad, and had financed one small war, the war for Cuba's sugar industry in 1898, but it did not feel capable of mortgaging itself to make national loans. The system of national loans which was perfected by the Rothschilds during the Napoleonic Wars served to finance Continental struggles throughout the nineteenth century, and also financed the South during the American Civil War. These national loans were made possible by the international financial organization of the Rothschild brothers, which had set up branches in all the major cities of Europe. Thus, the risk of any loan could be spread out, and profits also, and an international set-up reduced the possibility of governmental interference or control in any country.

By 1900, it had became apparent that the European countries could not afford a major war. They had large standing armies, universal military service, and central banks which could finance a war, but their economies could not afford it. As early as 1887, the editors of the Quarterly Journal of Economics in the April, 1887 issue, had pointed out that:

"A detailed revue of the public debts of Europe shows interest and sinking fund payments of $5,343 million annually (5 and 1/3 billion). M. Neymarck's conclusion is much like Mr. Atkinson's. The finances of Europe are so involved that the governments may ask whether war, with all its terrible chances, is not preferable to the maintainance of such a precarious and costly peace. If the military preparations of Europe do not end in war, they may well end in the bankruptcy of the States. Or, if such follies lead neither to war nor to ruin, then they assuredly point to industrial and economic revolution."

The First World War started in 1914. The Federal Reserve Banks began operation in 1914. The System forced the American people to lend the Allies twenty-five billion dollars which was not repaid, except in interest to the New York bankers, and it also committed us to make war against the German people, with whom we had no conceivable political or economic quarrel. The German Ambassador to Turkey, Baron Wangenheim, asked Henry Morgenthau, American Ambassador to Turkey, why the United States intended to make war upon Germany, since they both knew that there were no grounds for such aggression. "We Americans", replied Morgenthau, speaking, presumably, for that group of Harlem real estate operators of which he was head, "We Americans are going to war for a moral principle." That moral principle had a good amount of gold hidden in it. Mr. Morgenthau's moral principles had come to him from the New York slums which he ha drented to poor Negroes at high prices. A further study of the moral principles which activated the entry of the United States into the First World War reveals the Duponts doubling the price of their gunpowder to the government after the declaration of war, and J. P. Morgan Co. receiving the proceeds of the first Liberty Loan to pay off a $400,000,000 debt owed by Great Britain.

Woodrow Wilson's unofficial messenger and confidante during the entire time of his reign was Colonel House, who was sent to him with the cordial recommendations of Paul Warburg. Colonel House functioned as Wilson's private emissary to Europe for several years, keeping up the cordial relations between Felix and Paul Warburg of Kuhn, Loeb Co., New York, and the rest of the family in M. M. Warburg Co. of Amsterdam and Hamburg, including the brother who was head of the German secret service.

As we have stated, the United States prior to 1914 was a debtor nation. Most large national loans were floated with one or more of the important Rothschild affiliates in England, Frances, or Germany, the bulk of the loans being handled by the principal Rothschild agents in London, J. P. Morgan, Bliss, and Co., and J. P. Morgan, Drexel, and Co., which had offices in New York and London. The functions of these international companies were greatly lessened after 1914 when the Federal Reserve System took over the job of predetermining the rise or fall of security prices by raising or lowering the interest rate, and by dumping quantities of Government securities on the New York Stock Exchange. The New York Federal Reserve Bank under the guidance or Morgan employee Benjamin Strong cooperated closely with the Bank of England, and the Morgan houses suffered a great decline after 1914 in international finance. International financial relations are much eased by the existence of central banks in both countries concerned, and the League of Nations, after the war, was to prove its devotion to the interests which set it up, by refusing to make loans to nations which did not have a central bank, or which were not on the gold standard. The Rothschild-dominated Bank of England could now deal directly with its chief representative in the United States, Paul Warburg of the Rothschild-financed house of Kuhn, Loeb Co.

In 1915 and 1916, Woodrow Wilson kept faith with the bankers who had purchased the Presidency of the United States for him, by refusing to listen to the admonitions of his Secretary of State, William Jennings Bryan, against making loans to the Allies through the Rothschilds.

"Money" said Bryan, "is the worst of all contraband," and our loans to the Allies during the two and a half years before our entry into the First World War were more accurately acts of aggression than our belated shipments of troops in 1917, after Wilson's declaration of war had given an air of legality to the farce. By 1917, the Morgans and Kuhn, Loeb Co., had floated a billion and a half dollars worth of loans to the Allies in bonds sold by the big financiers of New York. Those bankers spent hundreds of thousands of dollars to get us into the war, using publicity from the Commission for Relief in Belgium, which manufactured atrocity stories, and The League to Enforce Peace, a Carnegie organization which agitated for war. By sending shipload after shipload of munitions to England and France (Cleveland H. Dodge, Wilson's closest friend and backer, owned the Remington Arms Co. and the Winchester Arms Co.) we provoked Germany into sinking those munitions ships, and one such vessel, the Lusitania, was sunk. American lives were lost, but the goods on board, ammunition from Cleveland H. Dodge's plants, were paid for. This was nothing, however, to the American lives which would be thrown away in France or the fortunes which would be made from the deaths of our soldiers.

Walter Hines Page, Ambassador to Britain, had complained that he couldn't afford the position, and was forthwith given twenty-five thousand dollars a year spending money by Cleveland H. Dodge. Page was openly accused by H. L. Mencken of being a British agent in

1916. On March 5, 1917, Walter Hines Page sent a confidential letter to Woodrow Wilson. This letter stated that:

"I think that the pressure of this approaching crisis has gone beyond the ability of the Morgan Financial Agency for the British and French Governments. The need is becoming too great and urgent for any private agency to meet, for every such agency has to encounter jealousies of rivals and of sections. The greatest help we could give the Allies would be a credit. Our Government could make a large investment in a Franco-British loan or might guarantee such a loan. Unless we go to war with Germany, our Government, of course, cannot make such a direct grant of credit."

Within the month, Woodrow Wilson asked Congress for a declaration of war, to save American bankers from a billion and a half dollars loss, and to provide an outlet for armaments. The first Liberty Loan of 400 million dollars went to J. P. Morgan Co. for repayment of a British Loan, and this was only the beginning of the party. The bankers and their managers of heavy industry, transportation, and communications, flocked to Washington for a year and a half picnic while they spent twenty-five billion dollars of our money. This entire sum went to enterprises which they owned. The spectacle of Eugene Meyer, Jr., director of the War Finance Corporation, taking advantage of his appointment to sell himself million of dollars worth of Government securities, is an index to the intrigues of wartime Washington.

The actual inspiration of Page's letter to Wilson was the fact that the Rothschilds were becoming alarmed at the rate of Germany's military successes, and were fearing that Germany might win the war after all. The financial chaos introduced in Germany by their agents, the Warburg family, who were financing the Kaiser's war, and the position of Paul Warburg's brother as head of the German Secret Service, which enabled him to authorize Lenin's train to go through Germany to the Russian front and make the Bolshevik Revolution possible, did not materially affect the German military machine. The drastic step of American entry into the war was necessary to save the Rothschild's overextended loans and to move the risk of their private banking firms in France and England off onto the American people. The financial future of the United States was mortgaged to provide security for the Allied loans.

American heavy industry, according to Under-Secretary of the Navy Franklin D. Roosevelt, had been preparing for war for nearly a year. Both the Army and Navy Departments had been purchasing heavily of war supplies since early in 1916. Cordell Hull remarks in his Memoirs that:

"The conflict forced the further development of the income-tax principle. Aiming, as it did, at the one great untaxed source of revenue, the income-tax law had been enacted in the nick of time to

— 55 —

meet the demands of war. And the conflict also assisted the putting into effect of the Federal Reserve System, likewise in the nick of time."

The Notes of the Journal of Political Economy, October, 1917, state that:

"The effect of the war upon the business of the Federal Reserve Banks has required an immense development of the staffs of these banks, with a corresponding increase in expenses. Without, of course, being able to anticipate so early and extensive a demand for their services in this connection, the framers of the Federal Reserve Act had provided that the Federal Reserve Banks should act as fiscal agents of the Government."

Both Hull and the editors of the Journal of Political Economy regard it as a pleasant surprise that the Federal Reserve System and the First World War, both starting at the same time, should find themselves so well adapted for each other. Hull apparently does not understand that the primary function of the central bank mechanism is war finance.

On October 13, 1917, Woodrow Wilson made the following speech:

"It is manifestly imperative that there should be a complete mobilization of the banking reserves of the United States. The burden and the privilege (of the Allied loans) must be shared by every banking institution in the country. I believe that cooperation on the part of the banks is a patriotic duty at this time, and that membership in the federal reserve system is a distinct and significant evidence of patriotism."

Wilson's speech was occasioned by the fact that the state bank and trust companies were not joining the Federal Reserve System in the expected numbers. Kemmerer writes that:

"As fiscal agents of the Government, the federal reserve banks rendered the nation services of incalculable value after our entrance into the war. They aided greatly in the conservation of our gold resources, in the regulation of our foreign exchanges, and in the centralization and efficient utilization of our financial energies. One shudders when he thinks what might have happened if the war had found us with our former decentralized and antiquated banking system."

Mr. Kemmerer's shudders are wasted. If we had kept our antiquated banking system", we would never have been able to finance the Allies or enter the war ourselves.

Woodrow Wilson himself did not believe in his crusade to save the world for democracy. He later wrote that:

"The World War was a matter of economic rivalry."

On being questioned by Senator McCumber about the circumstances of our entry into the war, Wilson was asked, "Do you think if Germany had committed no act of war or no act of injustice against our citizens that we would have gotten into this war?"

"I do think so," Wilson replied.

"You think we would have gotten in anyway?" asked McCumber.

"I do," said Wilson.

Whatever his philosophical position about our war with Germany, Woodrow Wilson did turn over this country to the worst elements in it during the First World War. The American people were put in the hands of three dictators, all three being Wall Street gamblers who had never held any elective office in the United States. One was the son of an immigrant from Poland, one was the son of an immigrant from France, and one was a German immigrant who had been naturalized in 1911.

Bernard Baruch, Eugene Meyer, Jr., and Paul Warburg, all appointed by their stooge Wilson, exercised more direct power over the American people than any President, because back of these men was the strength of the financial oligarchy which had maintained undisputed sway in this country since 1863.

Bernard Baruch first attracted attention on Wall Street as early as 1890, when he was known as a bright young man who worked for A. A. Housman & Co., stockbrokers. He was recognized by such stock speculators as Thomas Fortune Ryan and Henry H. Rogers as an exceptionally able organizer of corporations, and in 1896 he organized the six principal tabacco companies of the United States into the Consolidated Tobacco Co., forcing James Duke of the American Tobacco Co. to enter into the gigantic tobacco trust. The second great trust which Baruch organized was the copper trust, set up for the Guggenheim family, who have dominated the copper industry of this country ever since. Baruch also made his first contact with the firm of Kuhn, Loeb Co., when he and Edward H. Harriman, front man for Jacob Schiff's successful campaign to win America's railways for the Rothschild family, combined their talents to gain control over the public transit systems of New York City.

Bernard Baruch and his brother Herman formed the firm of Baruch Brothers, bankers, in New York in 1901. In 1917, it was dissolved so that Bernard could take over the position of Chairman of the War Industries Board. It became Hentz Brothers, bankers, after 1917.

Baruch was reported in a "New Yorker" profile to have made a profit of seven hundred and fifty thousand dollars in one day out of United States Steel stock, after a phony peace rumor was planted in Washington. With the publication of the peace news, steel stock dropped sharply, and Baruch bought up as much as he wanted. He had contributed fifty thousand dollars to Woodrow Wilson's campaign in 1915, and as payment he received control of America's heavy industry.

In "Who's Who in American Jewry", Baruch mentions that he was a member of the Commission which did *all* purchasing for the Allies during the war. This is a characteristic bit of modesty. Bernard Baruch *was* the Commission. He spent the American taxpayers' money at the rate of ten billion dollars a year, and saw to it that the orders went to those firms in which he had more than a polite interest.

Bernard Baruch was also the dominant member of the Munitions Price-Fixing Committee. This meant that he set the prices at which the United States Government purchased war materials from Baruch-owned companies. However, it was as Chairman of the War Industries Board that Baruch exercised dictatorial powers over American manufacturers. At the Nye Committee Hearings in 1935, Baruch testified that:

"President Wilson gave me a letter authorizing me to take over any industry or plant. There was Judge Gary, President of United States Steel, whom we were having trouble with, and when I showed him that letter, he said, 'I guess we will have to fix this up,' and he did fix it up."

Woodrow Wilson repaid Baruch's fifty thousand dollars by putting the entire American Government back of his manipulations. However, there were members of Congress to whom he had not given fifty thousand dollars, and they demanded to know what his qualifications were, that he should be given life or death powers over American industry in time of war. He was not a manufacturer. he had scarcely ever been in a factory in his life. Called before a Congressional Committee, Bernard Baruch said his profession was "speculator". A Wall Street gambler was the Czar of American industry, appointed to that position by a man who was elected President on the slogan "He kept us out of war", and who promptly declared war to protect the Rothschilds from further endangering of their credit structure.

The second of the three emperors of the United States in 1917 was Eugene Meyer, Jr., son of the dominant partner in the international banking house of Paris and New York, Lazard Freres. Meyer and Baruch purchased the Alaska-Juneau gold mine together in 1915, and were partners in other financial ventures, so that Wilson's choice was a happy team. Meyer was appointed Chairman of the War Finance Corporation by Woodrow Wilson at the insistence of Baruch and William G. McAdoo, Kuhn, Loeb, employee who was Secretary of the Treasury. Meyer's family house of Lazard Freres specialized in international gold movements, and his ownership of the Alaska-Juneau mine and gold properties in South Africa made him an esteemed member of the select circle of international financiers. As Chairman of the War Finance Committee, he was in charge of disposing of large quantities of Government securities to business firms. Member banks of the Federal Reserve System were under the domination of Paul Warburg, but Meyer was handling war finance of those financial agencies and banks not under control of the System. Meyer used his position to sell himself, that is, Eugene Meyer, Jr., New York, millions of dollars worth of United States bonds.

At the Senate Investigation into Meyer's qualifications to be Governor of the Federal Reserve Board, on January 27, 1931, a position to which he was appointed by Herbert Hoover, an old friend from London, Senator Robert L. Owen, Chairman of the Senate Committee on Banking and Currency, established the fact that Meyer was a brother-in-law of George Blumenthal, a member of the firm of J. P. Morgan Co., agents of the Rothschilds. Further testimony revealed that under Meyer's direction, at least twenty-four million dollars worth of Liberty Bonds had been printed *in duplicate*, and that ten billion dollars worth of First War bonds had been surreptitiously destroyed. (House Report 1635, 68th Congress, 2nd Session.) While the books were being brought before the Committee, during their investigation, they discovered that the books were being taken back to the Treasury each night, and that alterations were being made in the permanent records. Despite this testimony by a number of Congressmen, Meyer's appointment to the Federal Reserve Board was upheld, and Hoover's judgment vindicated.

The third member of the Triumvirate which ruled this country during the First War was Paul Warburg, whom we have already discussed at some length. With regards to his military value to the United States during time of war, the following United States Naval Secret Service Report of December 12, 1918, on Mr. Warburg is as follows:

"WARBURG, PAUL, New York City. German, naturalized American citizen 1911, was decorated by the Kaiser in 1912, was vice-chairman of the Federal Reserve Board, handled large sums furnished by Germany for Lenin and Trotsky. Has a brother who is leader of the espionage system of Germany."

Paul Warburg remained financial dictator of the United States during the First World War until May, 1918. According to the New York Times, his letter of resignation stated that some objection had been made because he had a brother in the Swiss Secret Service. We were not at war with Switzerland. He did not dare admit that his brother was head of the German Secret Service at the same time he was on the Federal Reserve Board. In any case, a man who had been decorated by the Kaiser might be regarded with some suspicion, especially in view of the state of hysteria induced by anti-German propaganda in this country's leading newspapers in 1917 and 1918. Since he himself had been a German national, until a mere five years before the War, he would, under the liberal policies of a Franklin D. Roosevelt, have been subject to concentration camp discipline.

These three appointees of Woodrow Wilson controlled the financial and industrial structure of the United States during the First World War, Baruch controlled industry, Meyer controlled all money and credit not in the power of the Federal Reserve System, and Warburg was dictator of the nation's formal banking structure. Besides these men, a host of J. P. Morgan Co. and Kuhn, Loeb Co., partners, employees, and satellites came to Washington to administer the fate of the American people.

The Liberty Loans, which sold bonds to our citizens, were nominally in the jurisdiction of the United States Treasury, under the leadership of Wilson's Secretary of the Treasury, William G. McAdoo, whom Kuhn, Loeb Co. had placed in charge of the Hudson-Manhattan Railway Co. in 1902. Paul Warburg, of Kuhn, Loeb Co. had most of his firm with him in Washington during the War. Jerome Hanauer, partner in Kuhn, Loeb Co., was Assistant Secretary of the Treasury in charge of Liberty Loans. The two Under-Secretaries of the Treasury during the War were S. Parker Gilbert and Roscoe C. Leffingwell. Both Gilbert and Leffingwell came to the Treasury from the law firm of Cravath and Henderson, and returned to that firm when they had fulfilled their mission for Kuhn, Loeb Co. in the Treasury. Cravath and Henderson were the lawyers for Kuhn, Loeb Co. Gilbert and Leffingwell subsequently received partnerships in J. P. Morgan Co.

One of the most mysterious events of the First World War was the appointment of the London mining promoter Herbert Hoover as United States Food Administrator by Woodrow Wilson. Even before Hoover had arrived in this country from his London home, even before Congress had heard of him, his secretary in the United States Food Administration, Lewis Lichtenstein Strauss, partner of Kuhn, Loeb So., and son-in-law of Jerome Hanauer of that firm, had already set up the Food Administrator's office and was issuing propaganda to the newspapers. A bewildered Congress okayed Wilson's appointment of Hoover as a matter of course, although it was thought to be somewhat improper for a man to open up shop before he had ever been mentioned for the job.

Kuhn, Loeb Company, the nation's largest owners of railroad properties in this country and in Mexico, protected their interests during the First World War by ordering Woodrow Wilson to set up a United States Railroad Administration. The Director-General was William McAdoo, and the Assistant Director-General was John Skelton Williams, Comptroller of the Currency. Warburg replaced this set up in 1918 with a tighter organization which he called the Federal Transportation Council. The purpose of both of these organizations was to prevent strikes against Kuhn, Loeb Co. during the war, in case the railroad workers should try to get in wages some of the millions of dollars in wartime profits which Kuhn, Loeb received from the United State Government.

Among the important bankers present in Washington during the War was Herbert Lehman, of the rapidly rising firm of Lehman Brothers, bankers New York. Lehman was promptly put on the General Staff of the Army, and presented with a Colonelcy.

Other appointments during the First World War were as follows:

J. W. McIntosh, director of the Armour meat-packing trust, who was made Chief of Subsistence for the United States Army in 1918. He later became Comptroller of the Currency during Coolidge's Administration, and ex-officio member of the Federal Reserve Board. During the Harding Administration, he did his bit as Director of Finance for the United States Shipping Board when the Board sold ships to the Dollar Lines for a hundredth of their cost and then let the Dollar Line default on its payments. After leaving public service, J. W. McIntosh became a partner in J. W. Wollman Co., New York stockbrokers.

W. P. G. Harding, Governor of the Federal Reserve Board, was also managing director of the War Finance Corporation under Eugene Meyer.

George R. James, member of the Federal Reserve Board in 1923-24, was Chief of the Cotton Section of the War Industries Board.

Henry P. Davison, senior partner in J. P. Morgan Co., was appointed head of the American Red Cross in 1917 in order to get control of the three hundred and seventy million dollars cash which was collected from the American people.

Ronald Ransom, banker from Atlanta, and Governor of the Federal Reserve Board under Roosevelt in 1938-39, was the Director in Charge of Personnel for Foreign Service for the American Red Cross in 1918.

John Skelton Williams, Comptroller of the Currency, was appointed National Treasurer of the American Red Cross.

President Woodrow Wilson, the great liberal who signed the Federal Reserve Act and declared war against Germany, had an odd career for a man who is now enshrined as a defender of the common people. His chief supporter in both his campaigns for the Presidency was Cleveland H. Dodge of the Kuhn, Loeb controlled National City Bank of New York, and President of the Winchester Arms Company and the Remington Arms Company. Dodge was very close to President Wilson throughout the great democrat's political career. Wilson lifted the embargo on shipment of arms to Mexico on February 12, 1914, so that Dodge could ship a million dollars worth of arms and ammunition to Carranza and promote the Mexican Revolution. Kuhn, Loeb Co., which owned the Mexican National Railways System, had become dissatisfied with the administration of Huerta and had him kicked out.

When the British naval auxiliary Lusitania was sunk in 1915, it was loaded with ammunition from Dodge's factories. Dodge became Chairman of the "Survivors of Victims of the Lusitania Fund", which did so much to arouse the public against Germany. Dodge also was notorious for using professional gangsters against strikers in his plants, yet the liberal Wilson does not appear to have ever been disturbed by this.

The key to Wilson's supposed liberalism, however, is to be found in Chaplin's book "Wobbly", which relates how Wilson scrawled the word "REFUSED" across the appeal for clemency sent him by the aging and ailing Eugene Debs, who had been sent to Atlanta Prison for "speaking and writing against war." The charge on which Debs was convicted was "spoken and written denunciation of war." This was treason to the Wilson dictatorship, and Debs was imprisoned. As head of the Socialist Party, Debs ran for the Presidency from Atlanta Prison, the only man ever to do so, and polled more than a million votes. It was ironic that Debs' leadership of the Socialist Party, which at that time represented the desires of many Americans for an honest government, should fall into the sickly hands of Norman Thomas, a former student and admirer of Woodrow Wilson at Princeton University. Under Thomas' leadership, the Socialist Party no longer stood for anything, and suffered a steady decline in influence and prestige.

The present-day admirers of Woodrow Wilson are led by the still omnipotent Bernard Baruch, who states that Woodrow Wilson was the greatest man he ever knew. Wilson's appointments to the Federal Reserve Board, and that body's responsibility for financing the First World War, as well as Wilson's handing over the United States to the immigrant Triumvir during the War, make him the most important single effector of ruin in American history.

It is no wonder that after his abortive trip to Europe, where he was hissed and jeered in the streets by the French people, and snickered at in the halls of Versailles by Orlando and Clemenceau, Woodrow Wilson returned home to take to his bed, a broken invalid. The sight of the destruction and death in Europe, for which he was directly responsible, was more of a shock than he could bear. The Italian Minister Pantaleoni expressed the feelings of the European peoples when he wrote that:

"Woodrow Wilson is a type of Pecksniff who was now disappeared amid universal execration."

It is America's misfortune that our subsidized press and educational system have been devoted to enshrining a man who colluded in causing so much death and sorrow throughout the world.

Chapter Nine
ALBERT STRAUSS

When Paul Warburg resigned from the Federal Reserve Board of Governors in 1918, his place was taken by Albert Strauss, partner in the international banking house of J. & W. Seligman. This banking house had large interests in Cuba and South America, and played a prominent part in financing the many revolutions in those countries. Its most notorious publicity came during the Senate Finance Committee's investigation of that firm in 1933, when it was brought out that J. & W. Seligman had given a $415,000 bribe to Juan Leguia, son of the President of Peru, in order to get that nation to accept a loan.

A partial list of Albert Strauss' directorships, according to "Who's Who in American Jewry", shows that he is:

Chairman of the Board of the Cuba Cane Sugar Corporation; Director, Brooklyn Manhattan Transit Co., Coney Island Brooklyn RR, New York Rapid Transit, Pierce-Arrow, Cuba Tobacco Corporation, and the Eastern Cuba Sugar Corporation.

Governor Delano resigned in August, 1918, to be commissioned a Colonel in the Army. The war ended on November 11, 1918.

William McAdoo was replaced in 1918 by Carter Glass as Secretary of the Treasury. Both Strauss and Glass were present during the secret meeting of the Federal Reserve Board on May 18, 1920, when the Agricultural Depression of 1920-21 was made possible.

One of the main lies about the Federal Reserve Act when it was being ballyhooed in 1931 was its promise to take care of the farmer. Actually, it has never taken care of anybody but a few big bankers. Prof. O. M. W. Sprague, Harvard economist, writing in the Quarterly Journal of Economics of February, 1914, said:

"The primary purpose of the Federal Reserve Act is to make sure that there will always be an available supply of money and credit in this country to meet unusual *banking* requirements." There is nothing there to help the farmer.

The First World War had introduced into this country a general prosperity, as revealed by the stocks of heavy industry on the New York Exchange in 1917-18, by the increase in the amount of money circulated, and by the enormous bank clearings during the whole of 1918. It was the assigned duty of the Federal Reserve System to get back the vast amount of money and credit which had escaped their control during this time of prosperity. This was done by the Agricultural Depression of 1920-21.

The open market operations of the Federal Reserve Open Market Committee in 1917-18, while Paul Warburg was still Chairman, show a tremendous increase in purchases of bankers' and trade acceptances. There was also a great increase in the purchase of United States Government securities, under the leadership of the able Eugene Meyer, Jr. A large part of the stock market speculation in 1919, at the end of the War when the market was very unsettled, was financed with funds borrowed from Federal Reserve Banks with Government securities as collateral. Thus the Federal Reserve System set up the

Depression, first by causing inflation, and then raising the discount rate and making money dear.

In 1914, Federal Reserve Bank rates had dropped from 6% to 4%, had gone to a further low of 3 percent in 1916, and had stayed at that level until 1920. The reason for the low interest rate was the necessity for floating the billion dollar Liberty Loans. At the beginning of each Liberty Loan Drive, the Federal Reserve Board put a hundred million dollars into the New York money market through its open market operations, in order to provide a cash impetus for the drive. The most important role of the Liberty Bonds was to soak up the increase in circulation of the medium of exchange (integer of account) brought about by the large amount of currency and credit put out during the war. Laborers were paid high wages, and farmers received the highest prices for their produce they had ever known. These two groups accumulated millions of dollars in cash which they did not put into Liberty Bonds. That money was effectively out of the hands of the Wall Street group which controlled the money and credit of the United States. They wanted it back, and that is why we had the Agricultural Depression of 1920-21.

Much of the money was deposited in the small country banks in the Middle West and West which had refused to have any part of the Federal Reserve System, the farmers and ranchers of those regions seeing no good reason why they should give a group of international financiers control of their money. The main job of the Federal Reserve System was to break these small country banks and get back the money which had been paid out to the farmers during the war, in effect, ruin them, and this it proceeded to do.

First of all, a Federal Farm Loan Board was set up which encouraged the farmers to invest their accrued money in land on long term loans, which the farmers were eager to do. Then inflation was allowed to take its course in this country and in Europe in 1919 and 1920. The purpose of the inflation in Europe was to cancel out a large portion of the war debts owed by the Allies to the American people, and its purpose in this country was to draw in the excess moneys which had been distributed to the working people in the form of higher wages and bonuses for production. As prices went higher and higher, the money which the workers had accumulated became worth less and less, thus inflicting upon them an unfair tax, while the propertied classes were enriched by the inflation because of the enormous increase in the value of land and manufactured goods. The workers were thus effectively impoverished, but the farmers, who were as a class more thrifty, and who were more self-sufficient, had to be handled more harshly.

G. W. Norris, in Collier's Magazine of March 20, 1920, said:

"Rumor has it that two members of the Federal Reserve Board had a plain talk with some New York bankers and financiers in

December, 1919. Immediately afterwards, there was a notable decline in transactions on the stock market and a cessation of company promotions. It is understood that action in the same general direction has already been taken in other sections of the country, as evidence of the abuse of the Federal Reserve System to promote speculation in land and commodities appeared.''

Senator Robert L. Owen, Chairman of the Senate Banking and Currency Committee, testified at the Senate Silver Hearings in 1939 that:

"In the early part of 1920, the farmers were exceedingly prosperous. They were paying off their mortgages and buying a lot of new land, at the instance of the Government—had borrowed money to do it—and then they were bankrupted by a sudden contraction of credit and currency which took place in 1920. What took place in 1920 was just the reverse of what should have been taking place. Instead of liquidating the excess of credits created by the war through a period of years, the Federal Reserve Board met in a meeting which was not disclosed to the public. They met on the 18th of May, 1920, and it was a secret meeting. They spent all day conferring; the minutes made sixty printed pages, and they appear in Senate Document 310 of February 19, 1923. The Class A Directors, the Federal Reserve Advisory Council, were present, but the Class B Directors, who represented business, commerce, and agriculture, were not present. The Class C Directors, representing the people of the United States, were not present and were not invited to be present. Only the big bankers were there, and their work of that day resulted in a contraction of credit which had the effect the next year of reducing the national income fifteen billion dollars, throwing millions of people out of employment, and reducing the value of lands and ranches by twenty billion dollars.''

Carter Glass, member of the Board in 1920 as Secretary of the Treasury, wrote in his autobiography, "Adventure in Constructive Finance", published in 1928, in response to criticism of his part in causing the Agricultural Depression by raising the discount rate to 7% on agricultural and livestock paper, said:

"Reporters were not present, of course, as they should not have been and as they never are at any bank board meeting in the world.''

It was Carter Glass who had complained that, if a suggested amendment by Senator LaFollette were passed, on the Federal Reserve Act of 1913, to the effect that no member of the Federal Reserve Board should be an official or director or stockholder of any bank, trust company, or insurance company, we would end up by having mechanics and farm laborers on the Board. Certainly mechanics and farm laborers could have caused no more damage to the country than did Glass, Strauss, and Warburg at the secret meeting of the Federal Reserve Board.

Senator Brookhart of Iowa testified that at that secret meeting of the Federal Reserve Board, Paul Warburg, then President of the Federal Advisory Board, which made the decisions for the Board, had a resolution passed to send a committee of five to the Interstate Commerce Commission and ask for an increase in railroad rates. As head of Kuhn, Loeb Co. which owned most of the railway mileage in the United States, he was already missing the huge profits which the United States Government had paid him during the war, and he wanted to inflict new price raises on the American people.

Senator Brookhart also testified that:

'I went into Myron T. Herrick's office in Paris, and told him that I came there to study cooperative banking. He said to me, 'As you go over the countries of Europe, you will find that the United States is the only civilized country in the world that by law is prohibiting its people from organizing a cooperative system.' I went up to New York and talked to about two hundred people. After talking cooperation and standing around waiting for my train—I did not specifically mention cooperative banking, it was cooperation in general—a man called me off to one side and said, 'I think Paul Warburg is the greatest financier we have ever produced. He believes a lot more of your cooperative ideas than you think he does, and if you want to consult anybody about the business of cooperation, he is the man to consult, because he believes in you, and you can rely on him.' A few minutes later I was steered up against Mr. Warburg himself, and he said to me, 'You are absolutely right about this cooperative idea. I want to let you know that the big bankers are with you. I want to let you know that now, so that you will not start anything on cooperative banking and turn them against you.' I said, 'Mr. Warburg, I have already prepared and tomorrow I am going to offer an amendment to the Lant Bill authorizing the establishment of cooperative national banks.' That was the intermediate credit act which was then pending to authorize the establishment of cooperative national banks. That was the extent of my conversation with Mr. Warburg, and we have not had any since.''

Mr. Wingo testified that in April, May, June, and July of 1920, the manufacturers and merchants were allowed a very large increase in credits. This was to tide them through the contraction of credit which was intended to ruin the American farmers, who, during this period, were denied all credit.

At the Senate Hearings in 1923, Eugene Meyer, Jr. put his finger on a primary reason for the Federal Reserve Board's action in raising the interest rate to 7% on agricultural and livestock paper:

"I believe," he said, "that a great deal of trouble would have been avoided if a larger number of the eligible non-member banks had been members of the Federal Reserve System." Meyer was correct in pointing this out. The purpose of the Board's action was to break those state and joint land-stock banks which had steadfastly refused to surrender their freedom to the banker's dictatorship set up by the System. Kemmerer in the "A B C of the Federal Reserve System" had written in 1919, that:

"The tendency will be toward unification and simplicity which will be brought about by the state institutions, in increasing numbers, becoming stockholders and depositors in the reserve banks." However, the state banks had not responded.

The Senate Hearings of 1923 into the causes of the Agricultural Depression of 1920-21 had been demanded by the American people. The complete record of the secret meeting of the Federal Reserve Board on May 18, 1920 had been printed in the "Manufacturers' Record" of Baltimore, Maryland, a magazine devoted to the interests of small Southern manufacturers.

Frank Vanderlip testified at these Hearings that not only had state banks failed to join in anticipated numbers after the passage of the Federal Reserve Act in 1913, but that during the war many of them dropped out. Thus, the Board's action continued that war against the rural banks which had been occasioned by the initial opposition of those banks to the Wall Street plan which Paul Warburg wrote for the House and which was signed by Woodrow Wilson. Andrew Frame had aroused the hatred of the New York bankers when he fought the Reserve Plan, and this hatred had first manifested itself in the distribution of the Reserve Banks so that the West was left without representation, and continued with the rate policy of the Board in 1920. The violent contraction of credit on May 18, 1920 ruined many western bankers.

Benjamin Marsh, Director of the Farmers' Council, testified that:

"Anything which turns over to private banks the issuance of credit is unconstitutional.

SENATOR GLASS: You think cooperative associations ought to be allowed to issue credit?

MARSH: Let them issue credit to their own members.

SENATOR GLASS: Do you think that the cooperative associations ought to be allowed to issue currency?

MARSH: No, let the Government issue currency, but not upon that fictitious and fluctuating value known as the gold standard.

SENATOR GLASS: Do you believe that the Federal Farm Loan Act has resulted in an orgy of land speculation?

MARSH: It is encouraging it. The financial interest tried to crush labor by the open-shop drive, and by breaking down immigration restrictions. Then they said, 'We have got to freeze millions of farmers off of their farms; let them go into industry and they will smash labor's standard.' Secretary of Agriculture Wallace (father of Henry Agard) has stated with great frankness that driving farmers off of the farms will result in restoring the parity between the prices which farmers get for their products, and the wages of labor."

Benjamin Strong, Governor of the Federal Reserve Bank of New York, and close friend of Montagu Norman, Governor of the Bank of England, said at these Hearings:

"The Federal Reserve System has done more for the farmer than he has yet begun to realize."

Emmanuel Goldenweiser, Director of Research for the Board of Governors, claimed that the discount rate was raised purely as an anti-inflationary measure, but he failed to explain why it was a raise aimed solely at farmers and workers, and at the same time the System protected the manufacturers and merchants by assuring them increased credits.

The final statement on the Federal Reserve Board's causing the Agricultural Depression of 1920-21 was made by William Jennings Bryan. In Hearst's Magazine of November 1923, he wrote:

"The Federal Reserve Bank that should have been the farmer's greatest protection has become his greatest foe. The deflation of the farmer was a crime deliberately committed."

Chapter Ten
MORE PAUL WARBURG

After the Agricultural Depression of 1920-21, the Federal Reserve Board of Governors settled down to a steady eight years of providing credit expansion for the New York bankers, a policy which culminated in the Great Depression of 1929-31 and paralyzed the economic structure of the world. Paul Warburg had resigned in May, 1918, after the monetary system of the United States had been changed from a bond-secured currency to a currency based upon commercial paper and the shares of the Federal Reserve Banks. Warburg returned to his five hundred thousand dollar a year job with Kuhn, Loeb Co., but he continued to determine the policy of the Federal Reserve System, as President of the Federal Advisory Council and as Chairman of the Executive Committee of the American Acceptance Council.

From 1921 to 1929, Paul Warburg organized three of the greatest trusts in the United States, the International Acceptance Bank, largest acceptance bank in the world, Agfa Ansco Film Corporation, with headquarters in Belgium, and I. G. Farben Corporation, whose American branch Warburg set up as American I. G. Chemical Corporation. A co-director in these enterprises was Bronson Winthrop, law partner of Henry L. Stimson, while Stimson continued to devote his life to public service.

In the early 1920s, the Federal Reserve System played the decisive role in the re-entry of Russia into the international finance structure. Winthrop and Stimson continued to be the correspondents between Russian and American bankers, and Henry L. Stimson handled the negotiations concluding in our recognition of the Soviet after Roosevelt's election in 1932. This was an anti-climax, because we had long before resumed exchange relations with Russian financiers.

The Federal Reserve System began purchasing Russian gold in 1920, and Russian currency was accepted on the Exchanges. According to Colonel Ely Garrison, in his autobiography, and according to the United States Naval Secret Service Report on Paul Warburg, the Russian Revolution had been financed by the Rothschilds and Warburgs, with a member of the Warburg family carrying the actual funds used by Lenin and Trotsky in Stockholm in 1918. This would theoretically place Russia outside the pale of international finance.

An article in the English monthly, "Fortnightly", July, 1922, says:

"During the past year, practically every single capitalistic institution has been restored. This is true of the State Bank, private banking, the Stock Exchange, the right to possess money to unlimited amount, the right of inheritance, the bill of exchange system, and other institutions and practices involved in the conduct of private industry and trade. A great part of the former nationalized industries are now found in semi-independent trusts."

The organization of powerful trusts in Russia under the guise of Communism made possible the sending of large amounts of financial and technical help from the United States. The Russian aristocracy had been wiped out because it was too inefficient to manage a modern industrial state. The international financiers provided funds for Lenin and Trotsky to overthrow the Czarist regime and keep Russia in the First World War. Peter Drucker, spokesman for the oligarchy in America, declared in an article in the Saturday Evening Post in 1948, that:

"RUSSIA IS THE IDEAL OF THE MANAGED ECONOMY TOWARDS WHICH WE ARE MOVING."

In Russia, the issuance of sufficient currency to handle the needs of their economy occurred only after a government had been put in power which had absolute control of the people. During the 1920s, Russia issued large quantities of so-called "inflation money", a managed currency. The same Fortnightly article (of July 1922) observed that:

"As economic pressure produced the "astronomical-dimensions system" of currency; it can never destroy it. Taken alone, the system is self-contained, logically perfected, even intelligent. And it can perish only through collapse or destruction of the political edifice which it decorates."

Fortnightly also remarked, in 1929, that:

"Since 1921 ,the daily life of the Soviet citizen is no different from that of the American citizen, and the Soviet system of government is more economical."

Admiral Kolchak. leader of the White Russian armies, was for awhile supported by the international bankers, who sent British and American troops to Siberia in order to have a pretext for printing Kolchak rubles. At one time in 1920, the bankers were manipulating on the London Exchange the old Czarist rubles, Kerensky rubles and Kolchak rbules, the values of all three fluctuating according to the movements of the Allied troops aiding Kolchak. Kolchak also was in possession of considerable amounts of gold which had been seized by his armies. After his defeat, a trainload of this gold disappeared in Siberia. At the Senate Hearings in 1921 on the Federal Reserve System, it was brought out that the System had been receiving this gold. Congressman Dunbar questioned Governor W. P. G. Harding of the Federal Reserve Board as follows:

DUNBAR: "In other words, Russia is sending a great deal of gold to the European countries, which in turn send it to us?

HARDING: This is done to pay for the stuff bought in this country and to create dollar exchange.

DUNBAR: At the same time, that gold came from Russia through Europe?

HARDING: Some of it is thought to be Kolchak gold, coming through Siberia, but it is none of the Federal Reserve Banks' business. The Secretary of the Treasury has issued instructions to the assay office not to take any gold which does not bear the mint mark of a friendly nation."

Just what Governor Harding meant by " a friendly nation" is not clear. In 1921, we were not, militarily, at least, at war with any country. At any rate, Congress was already beginning to question the international gold dealings of the Federal Reserve System. Governor Harding could very well shrug his shoulders and say that it was none of the Federal Reserve Banks' business where the gold came from. Gold knows no nationality or race. The United States by law had ceased to be interested in where its gold came from in 1906, when Secretary of the Treasury Shaw made arrangements with several of the larger New York banks (ones in which he had interests) to purchase gold with advances of cash from the United States Treasury, which would then purchase the gold from these banks. The Treasury could then claim that it did not know where its gold came from, since their office only registers the bank from which it made the purchase. Since 1906, the Treasury has not known which of the international gold merchants it was buying its gold from.

The First World War changed the status of the United States from that of a debtor nation to the position of the world's greatest creditor nation, a title formerly occupied by England. Since debt is money, according to Governor Marriner Eccles of the Federal Reserve Board, this also made us the richest nation of the world. The war also caused the removal of the headquarters of the world's acceptance market from London to New York, and Paul Warburg became the most powerful trade acceptance banker in the world. The mainstay of the international financiers, however, remained the same. The gold standard was still the basis of foreign exchange, and the small group of internationals who owned the gold controlled the monetary systems of the Western nations.

The chief weapon of the gold standard bankers during the 1920s and the 1930s was the League of Nations. Through this institution, most of the democracies were forced to go back on the gold standard between 1924 and 1928. These countries needed money for reconstruction after the First World War, and the League of Nations was willing to oblige. The only conditions were that the applicant nation have a central bank and be on the gold standard. Loans were not granted where these conditions did not exist. Consequently, central banks were set up in many countries where they had not been known before, particularly in the South American nations. Paul Einzig, in the London Economist, writes that:

"The League of Nations and cooperation between central banks put Europe back on the gold standard. Although in most cases, it was the League Finance Committee that created the international loans, its work was largely inspired by the Bank of England. Post-war international cooperation also assumed the form of extremely close contact between central banks. There was regular international exchange of information, and important decisions, such as bank-rate changes, were usually communicated in advance to other leading central banks. The internationalization of finance since the war was also largely responsible for governments and central banks accumulating huge floating balances."

During the 1920s, the Federal Reserve System functioned as a central bank mechanism which provided the facilities for domestic credit expansion and for foreign loans. Much of the increased potential of American heavy industry had been used up in the First World War. With the coming of peace, however, our economy faced the twin problems of overproduction and distribution. The insufficient qauntity of integer of account (monetary unit) in the United States prevented its citizens from receiving the benefits of the increased production, and on many items the manufacturers were faced with the problems of market satiation. American bankers during this period found it more profitable to finance foreign markets than to finance consumption at home.

At the House Hearings on Senate Bill 2472 on September 19, 1919, Edmund Platt, Chairman of the House Banking and Currency Committee, said:

"Some time ago a young man came up to me who said he had been to Bulgaria, I believe it was, and sold a million dollars worth of beds. He wanted the United States Government to send the money over to Bulgaria to pay for those beds."

Senator Walter Edge, remarked:

"That is exactly the story you are going to be getting from the manufacturers of this country very soon." The manufacturers sold goods abroad during the 1920s, and the Federal Reserve System co-operated by helping to float billions of dollars of foreign loans in this country during the 1920s. Franklin D. Roosevelt played an important part in many of these transactions, as President of some of the loan companies, and as lawyer for them in his firm of Roosevelt and O'Connor. The Federal Reserve System by its discount rate and open market operations created easy money conditions and cheap money rates in the United States so that the American people would buy those bonds. The bonds subsequently defaulted and our citizens lost three dollars out of four which they had invested in them.

Professor Gustav Cassel wrote in 1928:

"The American dollar, not the gold standard, is the world's monetary standard. The American Federal Reserve Board has the power to determine the purchasing power of the dollar by making changes in the rate of discount, and thus controls the monetary standard of the world."

If this were true, the members of the Federal Reserve Board would be the most powerful financiers in the world. Occasionally their membership includes such influential men as Paul Warburg or Eugene Meyer, Jr., but usually they are a rubber-stamp committee for the Federal Advisory Board and the Wall Street bankers. There has been a great deal of secrecy surrounding the activities of the Federal Reserve System, and its employees are investigated thoroughly before being hired. The System has high standards as regards "loyalty" and "security."

The matter of changing the discount rate, for instance, has never been satisfactorily explained. Inquiry at the Federal Reserve Board in Washington elicited the reply that "the condition of the money market is the prime consideration behind changes in the rate." Since the money market is in New York, it needs no wild imagination to deduce that New York bankers are interested in changes of the rate and attempt to influence it.

Norman Lombard, in the periodical "World's Work", writes that:

"In their consideration and disposal of proposed changes of policy, the Federal Reserve Board should follow the procedure and ethics observed by our court of law. Suggestions that there should be a change of rate or that the Reserve Banks should buy or sell securities may come from anyone and with no formality or written argument. The suggestion may be made to a Governor or Director of the Federal Reserve System over the telephone or at his club over the luncheon table, or it may be made in the course of a casual call on a member of the Federal Reserve Board. The interests of the one proposing the change need not be revealed, and his name and any suggestions he makes are usually kept secret. If it concerns the matter of open market operations, the public has no inkling of the decision until the regular weekly statement appears, showing changes in the holdings of the Federal Reserve Banks. Meanwhile, there is no public discussion, there is no statement of the reasons for the decision, or of the names of those opposing or favoring it.''

The chances of the average citizen meeting a Governor of the Federal Reserve System at his club are slight.

The House Hearings on Stabilization of the Purchasing Power of the Dollar in 1928 proved conclusively that the Federal Reserve Board worked in close cooperation with the heads of European central banks, and that the Depression of 1929-31 was planned at a secret luncheon of the Federal Reserve Board and those heads of European central banks in 1927. The Board has never been responsible to the public for its decisions or actions.

The true allegiance of the members of the Federal Reserve Board has always been to the big bankers, and this has merely been carrying out their central bank duties. The three features of the central bank, its ownership by private stockholders who receive rent and profit for their use of the nation's credit, absolute control of the nation's financial resources, and mobilization of the nation's credit to finance foreigners, all were demonstrated by the Federal Reserve System during the first fifteen years of its operations.

R. H. Brand, Chairman of the Proceedings of the Chatham House Study Group on Gold, in England in 1930, stated that:

''The first and fundamental duty of every central bank is to maintain its currency at a par with gold. The second duty of a central bank should be to work the gold standard so as to harmonize as far as possible external with internal requirements. The third duty, of course, is that each central bank should do what it can to maintain stability in the value of gold itself, but that is not a problem which can be solved in any way by one central bank; it must be the work in cooperation of all central banks.''

Chairman Brand pointed out that the central banks, including the Federal Reserve System, had to work together to keep the world on the gold standard and to keep up the price of gold. The League of Nations was set up to carry out these two objectives.

Jeremiah Smith said that:

''Before the World War there was little coooperation between the central banks of the different countries. The Experts' Conference of 1929 set up the Bank for International Settlements. It is imperative

— 73 —

that an institution of this sort, which would be carrying on transactions in all the important money markets of the world, should be governed by public interest. These considerations suggested immediately that the appropriate agencies for appointing the directors of the International Bank were the central banks of issue of the different countries, for these banks are relatively free from government influence. The other important benefit to be expected from the establishment of the Bank for International Settlements lies in its furnishing a regular meeting-place for the representatives of central banks, where the common problems of world finance may be discussed in a broad-minded manner. The Bank should vastly increase the prospects for international cooperation in the field of finance. The United States Government has announced that it would have nothing to do *officially* with the Bank, although apparently it does not object to having individuals participate at their own risk in the enterprise, if they are associated in no way with the Government or the Federal Reserve System."

The Government's cool attitude towards the Bank for International Settlements was short-lived, for it soon maintained a Treasury representative at the Bank for International Settlements, H. Merle Cochran, who was special liason officer from the United States Embassy in Paris. The Bank soon became known as the "Central Bankers' Club", where they could discuss world finance in a broad-minded manner, relatively free from newspaper reporters or public-minded citizens. Paul Einzig points out that "Meetings between Central Bankers are always either concealed or given obviously untrue explanations." The Bank for International Settlements was an international hideaway for them.

Paul Warburg's original plan for the Federal Reserve System, which was presented to Congress as the Aldrich Plan, had provided for the System to have branches in the principal foreign countries. Congress refused to approve such a provision, not realizing the exigencies of international finance, but the League of Nations later remedied this lack by setting up central banks in many countries which did not have them. These central banks, particularly those in South America, worked so closely in cooperation with the Federal Reserve System that they were, in effect, branch banks of the System. The officials of the Department of State stationed in those countries have seen to it that these central banks did their job.

In its report for 1918, the Federal Reserve Bank of New York outlined the arrangements which it had made with foreign banks *on behalf of all reserve banks*, whether those reserve banks liked it or not. The Federal Reserve Bank of New York has always handled foreign correspondence with foreign central banks.

'The following relationships, with the approval of the Federal

Reserve Board, have been concluded between the Federal Reserve Bank of New York and foreign banks or governments:

BANK OF ENGLAND: This is an arrangement of a formal character, covered by written agreement, ratified by the directors of the two institutions, covering in detail the basis of the principal operations and making a very close, complete, and effective agency. The business thus far transacted has been very limited, but under the agreement can be extended whenever the need arises.

BANK OF FRANCE: A somewhat limited agreement has been effected with the Bank of France, which it is hoped and expected by both institutions will soon ripen into a closer relationship.

BANK OF ITALY: A mutual agreement has been entered into between this institution and the Federal Reserve Bank of New York, whereby each has appointed the other its correspondent. No business has been or is likely to be transacted between the two institutions as long as arrangements for dealing with exchange problems growing out of the war are dealt with by the Governments of the two nations.

BANK OF JAPAN: Mutual arrangements, similar to those established with the Bank of Italy, have been concluded with the Bank of Japan, and although no active business has yet been transacted, it is hoped that, as in the case of other foreign agents and correspondents, a more active relationship will develop when international commerce resumes its natural course.

PHILIPPINE NATIONAL BANK · In May, 1917, mutual agency appointments were effected between the Philippine National Bank and this bank, but as the former has an active branch of its own in New York, the relationship, while ready for operations at any time, is likely to be largely of an emergency character.

DE NEDERLANDSCHE BANK: During 1918, at the request of the Treasury Department, this bank opened a current account with de Nederlandsche Bank for the purpose of receiving therein, for the use of the Treasury Department, the proceeds in guilders of wheat and other commodities.

ARGENTINA: Early in 1918 an important arrangement was entered into between the United States and the Argentine Governments whereby by the Federal Reserve Bank of New York and the Banco de la Nacion appointed each other as correspondents, and the former undertook to receive deposits not exceeding $100,000,000 exportable in gold coin after the proclamation of peace and the deposit of over $16,000,000 in gold coin then on deposit, earmarked, in New York, and since then withdrawn and exported. The purpose of this agreement, which has proved successful in operation, was to stabilize the badly demoralized exchange situation between the two countries.

DE JAVASCHE BANK: The arrangement effected in April, relating to deposits in current account, investments, collections and the earmarking of gold, has continued in active operation. The Federal

Reserve Bank of New York has formally appointed de Javasche Bank its agent and correspondent in Java, and in turn has acted as New York agent and correspondent of de Javasche Bank."

The aforegoing are typical arrangements made by the Federal Reserve Bank of New York, acting as agent for the entire System, with foreign central banks. It has always kept considerable quantities of gold in its vaults in New York which is earmarked for various foreign central banks, and the sizes and importance of this gold, sometimes amounting to hundreds of millions of dollars, has made it appear somewhat improper to have international gold dealers such as Albert Strauss and Eugene Meyer, Jr. on the Federal Reserve Board of Governors.

Further proof of the international purposes of the Federal Reserve Act of 1913 is provided by the "Edge Amendment", of December 24, 1919, which authorizes the organization of corporations expressly for "engaging in international or foreign banking or other international or foreign financial operations, including the dealing in gold or bullion, and the holding of stock in foreign corporations." On commenting on this amendment, E. W. Kemmerer, economist from Princeton University, remarked that:

"The federal reserve system is proving to be a great influence in the internationalizing of American trade and American finance."

The historic fact that this internationalizing of American trade and American finance has been the direct cause for involving us in two world wars does not disturb Mr. Kemmerer or any other well-paid economist. There is plenty of evidence to prove how Paul Warburg used the Federal Reserve System as the instrument for getting trade acceptances adopted on a wide scale by American businessmen.

The use of trade acceptances, (which are the currency of international trade) by bankers and corporations in the United States prior to 1915 was practically unknown. The coming to power of the Federal Reserve System exactly parallels the increase in the use of acceptances in this country, nor is this a coincidence. The men who wanted the Federal Reserve System were the men who set up acceptance banks and profited by the use of acceptances. The leader of these men was Paul Warburg.

As early as 1910, the National Monetary Commission began to issue pamphlets and other propaganda urging bankers and businessmen in this country to adopt trade acceptances in their transactions. For three years the Commission carried on this campaign, and the Aldrich Plan, written mainly by Paul Warburg, and presented to Congress as the work of the Commission, included a broad provision authorizing the introduction and use of bankers' acceptances into the American system of commercial paper.

The Federal Reserve Act of 1913 as passed by Congress did not specifically authorize the use of acceptances, and the Federal Reserve Board in 1915 and 1916 defined "trade acceptance", further defined by Regulation A, Series of 1920, and further defined by Series 1924. One of the first official acts of the Board of Governors in 1914 was to grant acceptances a preferentially low rate of discount at Federal Reserve Banks. Since acceptances were not being used in this country at that time, no explanation of business exigency could be advanced for this action. It was apparent that someone in power on the Board of Governors wanted the adoptance of acceptances.

The National Bank Act of 1864, which was the determining financial authority of the United States until November, 1914, when it was replaced by the Federal Reserve Act, did not permit banks to lend their credit. Consequently, the power of banks to create money was greatly limited. We did not have a bank of issue, that is, a central bank, which could create money in large amounts. To get a central bank, the bankers forced money panic after money panic on the business people of the United States, by shipping gold out of the country, creating a money shortage, and then importing it back. After we got our central bank, the Federal Reserve System, there was no longer any need for a money panic, because the banks could create money. However, the panic as an instrument of power over the business and financial community was used again on two important occasions, in 1920, causing the Agricultural Depression, because state banks and trust companies had refused to join the Federal Reserve System, and in 1929, causing the Great Depression, which centralized *all* power in this country in the hands of a few great trusts.

A trade acceptance is a draft drawn by the seller of goods on the purchaser, and accepted by the purchaser, with a time of expiration stamped upon it. The use of trade acceptances in the wholesale market supplies short-term, assured credit to carry goods in process of production, storage, transit, and marketing. It facilitates domestic and foreign commerce. Seemingly, then, the bankers who wish to replace the open-book account system with the trade acceptance system were progressive-minded men who wished to help American import-export trade. Much propaganda was issued to that effect, but this was not the story.

The open-book system, heretofore used entirely by American business people, allowed a discount for cash. The acceptance system however, discourages the use of cash, by allowing a discount for credit. The open-book system also allowed much easier terms of payment, with liberal extensions on the debt. The acceptance does not allow this, since it is a short-term credit with the time-date stamped upon it. It is out of the seller's hands, and in the hands of a bank, usually an acceptance bank, which does not allow any extension of time. Thus, the adoption of acceptances by American businessmen during the 1920s greatly facilitated the domination and swallowing up of small business into huge trusts, which culminated in the crash of 1929.

Trade acceptances had been used to some extent in the United States before the Civil War. During that war, exigencies of trade had destroyed the acceptance as a credit medium, and it had not come back into favor in this country, our people preferring the simplicity and generosity of the open book system. Open-book accounts are single-name commercial paper, bearing only the name of the debtor. Acceptances are two-name paper, bearing the name of the debtor *and* the creditor. Thus they are much more acceptable by banks. To the creditor, under the open-book system, the debt is a liability. To the acceptance bank holding an acceptance, the debt is an asset. The men who set up acceptance banks in this country, under the leadership of Paul Warburg, secured control of the billions of dollars of credit existing as open accounts on the books of American businessmen.

Governor Marriner Eccles of the Federal Reserve Board stated before the House Banking and Currency Committee that:

"Debt is the basis for the creation of money."

The holders of trade acceptances got the use of billions of dollars worth of credit-money, besides the rate of interest charged upon the acceptance itself. It is understandable why Paul Warburg should have devoted so much time, money, and energy to getting acceptances adopted in this country.

On September 4, 1914, the National City Bank accepted the first timedraft drawn on a national bank under provisions of the Federal Reserve Act of 1913. This was the beginning of the end of the open-book account system as an important factor in wholesale trade. Beverly Harris, vice-president of the National City Bank of New York, issued a pamphlet in 1915 stating that:

"Merchants using the open account system are usurping the functions of bankers."

This was a plain statement of the purpose of Warburg and his bunch who wanted "monetary reform" in this country. They were out to get control of all credit in the United States, and they got it, by means of the Federal Reserve System and the acceptance system.

The First World War was a boon to the introduction of trade acceptances, and the volume jumped to four hundred million dollars in 1917, growing through the 1920s to more than a billion dollars a year, which culminated in a high peak just before the Great Depression of 1929-31. The Federal Reserve Bank of New York's charts show that its use of acceptances reached a peak in November 1929, the month of the stock market crash, an declined sharply thereafter. The acceptance people had got what they wanted, which was control of American business and industry. Fortune Magazine in February of 1950 pointed out that:

"Volume of acceptances declined from $1,732 million in 1929 to $209 million in 1940, because of the concentration of acceptance banking in a few hands, and the Treasury's low-interest policy, which made direct loans cheaper than acceptance. There has been a slight upturn since the war, but it is often cheaper for large companies to finance imports from their own coffers.''

In other words, the "large companies", more accurately, the great trusts, now have control of credit and have not needed acceptances. Their use did not increase rapidly among American businessmen, and a great deal of propaganda was necessary to foster them. Besides the barrage of propaganda issued by the Federal Reserve System itself, the National Association of Credit Men, the American Bankers' Association, and other fraternal organizations of the New York bankers devoted much time and money to distributing acceptance propaganda. Even their flood of lectures and pamphlets proved insufficient, and in 1919 Paul Warburg organized the American Acceptance Council, which was devoted entirely to acceptance propaganda.

The first convention held by this association at Detroit, Michigan, on June 9, 1919, coincided with the annual convention of the National Association of Credit Men, held there on that date, so that "interested observers might with facility participate in the lectures and meetings of both groups,'' according to a pamphlet issue by the American Acceptance Council.

Paul Warburg was elected President of this organization, and later became Chairman of the Executive Committee of the American Acceptance Council, a position which he held until his death in 1932. The Council published lists of corporations using trade acceptances, all of them businesses in which Kuhn, Loeb Co. or its affiliates held control. Lectures given before the Council or by members of the Council were attractively bound and distributed free by the National City Bank of New York to the country's businessmen.

Louis T. McFadden, Chairman of the House Banking and Currency Committee, charged in 1922 that the American Acceptance Council was exercising undue influence on the Federal Reserve Board, and called for a Congressional investigation, but Congress was not interested.

At the second annual convention of the American Acceptance Council, held in New York on December 2, 1920, President Paul Warburg stated:

"It is a great satisfaction to report that during the year under review it was possible for the American Acceptance Council to further develop and strengthen its relations with the Federal Reserve Board.''

During the 1920s, Paul Warburg, who had resigned from the Federal Reserve Board after holding a position as Governor for a year in wartime, because his brother was head of the German Secret Service, continued to exercise direct personal influence on the Federal Reserve Board by meeting with the Board as President of the Federal

Advisory Board and as President of the American Acceptance Council. He was, from its organization in 1920 until his death in 1932, Chairman of the Board of the International Acceptance Bank of New York, the largest acceptance bank in the world. His brother, Felix M. Warburg, also a partner in Kuhn, Loeb Co., was director of the International Acceptance Bank, and Paul's son, James Paul Warburg, was Vice-President. Paul Warburg was also a director on other important acceptance banks in this country, such as the Westinghouse Acceptance Bank, which were organized in the United States immediately after the World War, when the headquarters of the international acceptance market was moved from London to New York, and Paul Warburg became the most powerful acceptance banker in the world.

It was the transference of the acceptance market from England to this country which gave rise to Thomas Lamont's ecstatic speech before the Academy of Political Science in 1917 that:

"The dollar, not the pound, is now the basis for international exchange."

Visible proof of the undue influence of the American Acceptance Council on the Federal Reserve Board, about which Congressman McFadden complained, is the chart showing the rate-pattern of the Federal Reserve Bank of New York during the 1920s. The Bank's official discount rate follows exactly for nine years the ninety-day bankers' acceptance rate, and the Federal Reserve Bank of New York sets the discount rate for the rest of the Reserve Banks. During this period, other rates of this Bank, such as the call-money rate, show remarkable variations, but the official rate and the acceptance. rate move along as one.

Chapter Eleven
ANDREW MELLON

In 1921, President Harding was praised for securing Andrew Mellon's services as Secretary of the Treasury. Mr. Mellon was a member of the infamous "Black Cabinet", two members of which were indicted and prosecuted for defrauding the United States of America, Attorney General Harry M. Daugherty, and Secretary of the Interior Albert Fall. Assistant Secretary of the Navy Theodore Roosevelt, Jr., son of the twenty-sixth President of the United States, was the man who persuaded President Harding to sign the papers turning over the hundred million dollar oil reserves of Teapot Dome to Roosevelt's employer, Harry Sinclair. Roosevelt had been a director in the Sinclair Oil Company. His brother Archibald was a director of the Sinclair Oil Company at the time of this swindle, yet Roosevelt was never indicted for his key role in this criminal conspiracy against the people of the United States. Andrew Mellon during his decade as Secretary of the Treasury surpassed all these men in the enormity of his frauds against the American people. As an ex-officio member of the Federal Reserve Board, he abetted in the credit expansion of the 1920s which culminated in the Great Depression of 1929-31, but he was far more culpable and subject to prosecution for his outrageous tax rebate policy during his term of office. He returned to such big corporations as United States Steel, in which he was a dominant partner, more than twenty billions of dollars in tax rebates, including all the corporate taxes which United States Steel had paid in 1917 and 1918 on its enormous wartime profits during the First World War. Andrew Mellon was one of the ten richest men in the country, and for power in finance and industry there was none to surpass him except Paul Warburg. Andrew Mellon was the biggest banker in Pennsylvania, and he owned outright such immense corporations as Aluminum Corp. of America. He was partner with Henry Frick in Frick's coke-processing patents, and he was partner with Bernard Baruch in many enterprises. It was Mellon's brother Richard who had won a sort of fame for his remark that:

"You can't run a coal mine without machine guns."

Andrew Mellon reluctantly relinquished the office of Secretary of the Treasury in 1932 after there had been repeated demands in Congress for his impeachment on the grounds of his tax rebate policy to Mellon family corporations. He was succeeded by a man after his own heart, Ogden Mills, director of many giant corporations such as Cerro de Pasco Copper Mines of Peru, National Biscuit Company, and Morgenthaler Linotype Company.

Other members of the Federal Reserve Board during the 1920s, when it planned and executed the Great Depression as a deliberate means of gaining control over American finance and industry, were men like Albert Strauss, J. &. W. Seligman Company of New York and Paris, who had large interests in Cuban sugar and New York subways.

Edmund Platt, former Chairman of the House Committee on Banking and Currency, who was appointed in 1920, and who resigned in 1930 just after being appointed to a second ten-year term. He was given a position as Vice-President of the Marine Midland Corporation, in order to make room on the Federal Reserve Board for Eugene Meyer, Jr.

D. R. Crissinger, Comptroller of the Currency for Harding, an old friend from Marion, Ohio, was one of the famous poker-playing cronies of the President.

George R. James was appointed member of the Board of Governors in 1924. He had been Chief of the Cotton Section of the War Industries Board under Bernard Baruch during the First World War, and could be depended upon to follow that great democrat's orders.

David C. Wills had been appointed member of the Board of Governors in 1920. He was a Vice-President of the Mellon National Bank in Pittsburgh, and went back to that job after his term of public service.

Henry M. Dawes, who represented big public utility interests in Chicago, served as Comptroller of the Currency in 1923.

J. W. McIntosh replaced Dawes as Comptroller of the Currency in 1924. He resigned in 1928 to become a member of the firm of J. W. Wollman Company, stock brokers, New York.

R. A. Young, Governor of the Federal Reserve Bank of Minneapolis, joined the Federal Reserve Board of Governors in 1927. In 1930, after playing his part in the Great Depression, he was advanced to the position of Governor of the Federal Reserve Bank of Boston.

During the 1920s, the Board of Governors retained two of its first members, C. S. Hamlin and Adolph C. Miller. These men found themselves careers as arbiters of the nation's monetary policy. Hamlin was on the Board from 1914 until 1936, when he was appointed Special Counsel to the Board, while Miller served from 1914 until 1931. These two men were allowed to stay on the Board so many years because they were both eminently respectable men who gave the Board a certain prestige in the eyes of the public, and to those names no stigma of materialist motives could be attached. This was necessary during these years, when one big banker after another came on the Board, served for awhile, and went on to better things. Neither Miller nor Hamlin ever objected to anything that the New York bankers wanted. They changed the discount rate and they performed open market operation with Government securities whenever Wall Street wanted them to. Behind them throughout the 1920s was the figure of Paul Warburg, who exercised a continuous and dominant influence as President of the Federal Advisory Council, on which he had such men of common interests with himself as Winthrop Aldrich and J. P. Morgan, and as Chairman of the Executive Committee of the American Acceptance Council. Warburg was never too occupied with his duties of organizing such big international trusts as I. G. Farben, Westinghouse Corporation, and Agfa Ansco Film Corporation, to keep his hands off the nation's financial structures. His influence from 1902, when he arrived in this country as an immigrant from Germany, until 1932, the year of his death, was undoubtedly the most sinister and destructive influence ever foisted on the American people, even exceeding that of his puppet Woodrow Wilson and the international bond promoter Franklin D. Roosevelt. Warburg's son, James Paul Warburg, continued to exercise such influence, being appointed Roosevelt's Director of the Budget when that great man assumed office in 1933, and setting up the Office of War Information, our official propaganda agency during the Second World War. Warburg the Second remains a potent influence on the foreign policy of the United States.

The international gold dealings of the Federal Reserve System, and its active support in helping the League of Nations to force all the nations of Europe and South America back on the gold standard for the benefit of international gold merchants like Eugene Meyer, Jr. and Albert Strauss, is best demonstrated by a classic incident, the sterling credit of 1925.

J. E. Darling wrote, in the English periodical, "Spectator", on January 10, 1925, that:

"Obviously, it is of the first importance to the United States to induce England to resume the gold standard as early as possible. An American controlled Gold Standard, which must inevitably result in the United States becoming the world's supreme financial power, makes England a tributary and satellite, and New York the world's financial centre."

Mr. Darling fails to point out that the American people have as little to do with this as the British people, and that resumption of the gold standard by Britain would benefit only that small group of international gold merchants who own the world's gold. No wonder that Banker's Magazine gleefully remarked in July, 1925 that:

"The outstanding event of the past half year in the banking world was the restoration of the gold standard."

In May, 1925, the British Parliament passed the Gold Standard Act, putting Great Britain back on the gold standard. The Federal Reserve System's major role in this event came out on March 16, 1926, when George Seay, Governor of the Federal Reserve Bank of Richmond, testified before the House Banking and Currency Committee that:

"A verbal understanding, confirmed by correspondence, extended Great Britain a two hundred million dollar gold loan or credit. All negotiations were conducted between Benjamin Strong, Governor of the Federal Reserve Bank of New York, and Mr. Montagu Norman, Governor of the Bank of England. The purpose of this loan was to help England get back on the gold standard, and the loan was to be met by investment of Federal Reserve funds in bills of exchange and foreign securities."

The Federal Reserve Bulletin of June, 1925, stated that:

"Under its arrangement with the Bank of England the Federal Reserve Bank of New York undertakes to sell gold on credit to the Bank of England from time to time during the next two years, but not to exceed $200,000,000 outstanding at any one time."

A two hundred million dollar gold credit had been arranged by a verbal understanding between the international bankers, Benjamin Strong and Montagu Norman. It was apparent by this time that the Federal Reserve System had other interests at heart than the financial needs of American business and industry. Great Britain's return to the gold standard was further facilitated by an additional gold loan of a hundred million dollars from J. P. Morgan Company. Winston

Churchill, British Chancellor of the Exchequer, complained later that the cost to the British Government of this loan was $1,125,000 the first year, this sum representing the profit to J. P. Morgan Company in that time.

In "The Fight for Financial Supremacy," Macmillan's, 1931, Paul Einzig, editorial writer for the London Economist, wrote that:

"Almost immediately after World War I a close cooperation was established between the Bank of England and the Federal Reserve authorities, and more especially with the Federal Reserve Bank of New York. This cooperation was largely due to the cordial relations existing between Mr. Montagu Norman of the Bank of England and Mr. Benjamin Strong, Governor of the Federal Reserve Bank of New York until 1928. On several occasions, the discount rate policy of the Federal Reserve Bank of New York was guided by a desire to help the Bank of England. There has been close cooperation in the fixing of discount rates between London and New York."

At the Senate Hearings on the Federal Reserve System in 1931, H. Parker Willis, one of the authors and First Secretary of the Federal Reserve Board from 1914 until 1920, pointedly asked Governor George Harrison, Strong's successor as Governor of the Federal Reserve Bank of New York:

"What is the relationship between the Federal Reserve Bank of New York and the money committee of the Stock Exchange?"

"There is no relationship" Governor Harrison replied.

"There is no assistance or cooperation in fixing the rate in any way?" asked Willis.

"No," said Governor Harrison, "although on various occasions they advise us of the state of the money situation, and what they think the rate ought to be." This was an absolute contradiction of his statement that "There is no relationship." The Federal Reserve Bank of New York, which set the discount rate for the other Reserve Banks, actually maintained a close liason with the money committee of the Stock Exchange.

The House Stabilization Hearings of 1928 proved conclusively that the Governors of the Federal Reserve System had been holding conferences with heads of the big European central banks. A number of Congressmen knew that something big was being planned, but how big it was and how shattering its effect would be, they had no conception. Even had they known the details of the plot which was to culminate in the Great Depression of 1929-31, there would have been absolutely nothing they could have done to stop it. The international bankers who controlled gold movements could inflict their will on any country, and the United States to them was as helpless as any other.

Notes from these House Hearings follow:

MR. BEEDY: "I notice on your chart that the lines which produce the most violent fluctuations are found under "Money Rates in New York." As the rates of money rise and fall in the big cities, the loans that are made on investments seem to take advantage of them, at present, a quite violent change, while industry in general does not seem to avail itself of these violent changes, and that line is fairly even, there being no great rises or declines.

GOVERNOR ADOLPH MILLER: This was all more or less in the interests of the international situation. They sold gold credits in New York for sterling balances in London.

REPRESENTATIVE STRONG (No relation to Benjamin): Has the Federal Reserve Board the power to attract gold to this country?

E. A. GOLDENWEISER, research director for the Board: The Federal Reserve Board could attract gold to this country by making money rates higher.

GOVERNOR ADOLPH MILLER: I think we are very close to the point where any further solicitude on our part for the monetary concerns of Europe can be altered. The Federal Reserve Board last summer, 1927, set out by a policy of open-market purchases, followed in course by reduction on the discount rate at the Reserve Banks, to ease the credit situation and to cheapen the cost of money. The official reasons for that departure in credit policy were that it would help to stabilize international exchange and stimulate the exportation of gold.

CHAIRMAN MCFADDEN: Will you tell us briefly how that matter was brought to the Federal Reserve Board and what were the influences that went into the final determination?

GOVERNOR ADOLPH MILLER: You are asking a question impossible for me to answer.

CHAIRMAN MCFADDEN: Perhaps I can clarify it—where did the suggestions come from that caused this decision of the change of rates last summer?

GOVERNOR ADOLPH MILLER: The three largest central banks in Europe had sent representatives to this country. There were the Governor of the Bank of England, Mr. Montagu Norman, the President of the German Reichsbank, Mr. Hjalmar Schacht, and Professor Rist, Deputy Governor of the Bank of France. These gentlemen were in conference with officials of the Federal Reserve Bank of New York. After a week or two, they appeared in Washington for the better part of a day. They came down the evening of one day, and were the guests of the Governors of the Federal Reserve Board the following day, and left that afternoon for New York.

CHAIRMAN MCFADDEN: Were the members of the Board present at this luncheon?

GOVERNOR ADOLPH MILLER: Oh, yes, it was given by

the Governors of the Board for the purpose of bringing all of us together.

CHAIRMAN MCFADDEN: Was it a social affair, or were matters of importance discussed?

GOVERNOR MILLER: I would say it was mainly a social affair. Personally, I had a long conversation with Dr. Schacht alone before the luncheon, and also one of considerable length with Professor Rist. After the luncheon I began a conversation with Mr. Norman, which was joined in by Governor Strong of New York.

CHAIRMAN MCFADDEN: Was that a formal meeting of the Board?

GOVERNOR ADOLPH MILLER: No.

CHAIRMAN MCFADDEN: It was just an informal discussion of the matters they had been discussing in New York?

GOVERNOR MILLER: I assume so. It was mainly a social occasion. What I said was mainly in the nature of generalities. The heads of these central banks also spoke in generalities.

MR. KING: What did they want?

GOVERNOR MILLER: They were very candid in answers to questions. I wanted to have a talk with Mr. Norman, and we both stayed behind after luncheon, and were joined by the other foreign representatives and the officials of the New York Reserve Bank. *These gentlemen were all pretty concerned with the way the gold standard was working.* They were therefore desirous of seeing an easy money market in New York and lower rates, which would deter gold from moving from Europe to this country. That would be very much in the interest of the international money situation which then existed.

MR. BEEDY: Was there some understanding arrived at between the representatives of these foreign banks and the Federal Reserve Board or the New York Federal Reserve Bank?

GOVERNOR MILLER: Yes.

MR. BEEDY: It was not reported formally?

GOVERNOR MILLER: No. Later, there came a meeting of the Open-Market Policy Committee, the investment policy committee of the Federal Reserve System, by which and to which certain recommendations were made. My recollection is that about eighty million dollars worth of securities were purchased in August consistent with this plan.

CHAIRMAN MCFADDEN: Was there any conference between the members of the Open-Market Committee and those bankers from abroad?

GOVERNOR MILLER: They may have met them as individuals, but not as a committee.

MR. KING: How does the Open-Market Committee get its ideas?

GOVERNOR MILLER: They sit around and talk about it. I

do not know whose idea this was. It was distinctly a time in which there was a cooperative spirit at work.

CHAIRMAN MCFADDEN: You have outlined here negotiations of very great importance.

GOVERNOR MILLER: I should rather say conversations.

CHAIRMAN MCFADDEN: Something of a very definite character took place?

GOVERNOR MILLER: Yes.

CHAIRMAN MCFADDEN: A change of policy on the part of our whole financial system which has resulted in one of the most unusual situations that has ever confronted this country financially (the stock market speculation boom of 1927-1929). It seems to me that a matter of that importance should have been made a matter of record in Washington.

GOVERNOR MILLER: I agree with you.

REPRESENTATIVE STRONG: Would it not have been a good thing if there had been a direction that those powers given to the Federal Reserve System should be used for the continued stabilization of the purchasing power of the American dollar rather than be influenced by the interests of Europe?

GOVERNOR MILLER: I take exception to that term 'influence.' Besides, there is no such thing as stabilizing the American dollar without stabilizing every other gold currency. They are tied together by the gold standard. Other eminent men who come here are very adroit in knowing how to approach the folk who make up the personnel of the Federal Reserve Board.

MR. STEAGALL: The visit of these foreign bankers resulted in money being cheaper in New York?

GOVERNOR MILLER: Yes, exactly

CHAIRMAN MCFADDEN: I would like to put in the record all who attended that luncheon in Washington.

GOVERNOR MILLER: In addition to the names I have given you, there was also present one of the younger men from the Bank of France. I think all members of the Federal Reserve Board were there. Under Secretary of the Treasury Ogden Mills was there, and the Assistant Secretary of the Treasury, Mr. Schuneman, also, two or three men from the State Department, and Mr. Warren of the Foreign Department of the Federal Reserve Bank of New York. Oh yes, Governor Strong was present.

CHAIRMAN MCFADDEN: This conference, of course, with all of these foreign bankers did not just happen. The prominent bankers from Germany, France, and England came here at whose suggestion?

GOVERNOR MILLER: A situation had been created that was distinctly embarrassing to London by reason of the impending withdrawal of a certain amount of gold which had been recovered by France and that had originally been shipped and deposited in the

Bank of England by the French Government as a war credit. There was getting to be some tension of mind in Europe because France was beginning to put her house in order for a *return to the gold standard*. The situation was one which called for some moderating influence.

MR. KING: Who was the moving spirit who got these people together?

GOVERNOR MILLER: That is a detail with which I am not familiar.

REPRESENTATIVE STRONG: Would it not be fair to say that the fellows who wanted the gold were the ones who instigated the meeting?

GOVERNOR MILLER: They came over here.

REPRESENTATIVE STRONG: The fact is that they came over here, they had a meeting, they banqueted, they talked, they got the Federal Reserve Board to lower the discount rate, and to make the purchases in the open market, and they got the gold.

MR. STEAGALL: Is it true that that action stabilized the European currencies, and upset ours?

GOVERNOR MILLER: *Yes, that was what it was intended to do.*

CHAIRMAN MCFADDEN: Let me call your attention to the recent conference in Paris at which Mr. Goldenweiser, director of research for the Federal Reserve Board, and Dr. Burgess, assistant Federal Reserve Agent of the Federal Reserve Bank of New York, were in consultation with the representatives of the other central banks. Who called that conference?

GOVERNOR MILLER: My recollection is that it was called by the Bank of France.

GOVERNOR YOUNG: No, it was the *League of Nations* who called them together.

GOVERNOR MILLER: The more scientific you undertake to make Federal Reserve administration, the more dependent you make the men charged with it upon their advisors. I am a great believer in experts, *when you know how to use them.* I had a visit yesterday afternoon from a New York banker who said, 'Why is there so much mystery about gold movements? We get figures of shipping permits but there seems to be a great mystery regarding the earmarking of gold.'

CHAIRMAN MCFADDEN (quoting from an article by H. Parker Willis in the Journal of Commerce, May 17, 1928, entitled International Bank Tinkering): "Ever since our Federal Reserve System was formed, it has suffered from back-stairs influences and behind-the-doors conferences. These conferences first aimed at the destruction of the authority of the Board itself, and gave rise to the famous 'council-of-governors' (Federal Advisory Council) whose doings never got into the newspapers."

Professor Gustav Cassel, the Scandinavian economist, testified at these Hearings, that:

"When you desire to stabilize the value of gold, you have to cooperate with other countries, and particularly with their central banks."

The secret meeting between the Governors of the Federal Reserve Board and the heads of the European central banks was not held to stabilize anything. It was held to discuss the best way of getting the gold held in the United States by the System back to Europe to get the nations of that continent back on the gold standard. The League of Nations had not yet succeeded in doing that, the objective for which that body was set up in the first place, mainly because the Senate of the United States had refused to let Woodrow Wilson betray us to an international monetary authority. It took the Second World War and Franklin D. Roosevelt to do that. Meanwhile, Europe had to have the gold which we had, and the Federal Reserve System gave it to them, five hundred million dollars worth. The movement of that gold out of the United States caused the deflation of the stock boom, the end of the business prosperity of the 1920s, and the Great Depression of 1929-31, the worst calamity which has ever befallen this nation. It is entirely logical to say that the American people suffered that depression as a consequence and a punishment for not wishing to join the League of Nations. The bankers knew what would happen when that five hundred million dollars worth of gold was sent to Europe. They wanted the Depression because it put the business and finance of the United States completely in their hands.

The Hearings continue:

MR. BEEDY: "Mr. Ebersole of the Treasury Department concluded his remarks at the dinner we attended last night by saying that the Federal Reserve System did not want stabilization and the American businessman did not want it. They want these fluctuations in prices, not only in securities but in commodities, in trade generally, because those who are now in control are making their profits out of that very instability. If control of these people does not come in a legitimate way, there may be an attempt to produce it by general upheavals such as have characterized society in days gone by. Revolutions have been promoted by dissatisfaction with existing conditions, the control being in the hands of the few, and the many paying the bills.

CHAIRMAN MCFADDEN: I have here a letter from a member of the Federal Reserve Board who was summoned to appear here. I would like to have it put in the record. It is from Governor Cunningham.

Dear Mr. Chairman:

For the past several weeks I have been confined to my home on account of illness and am now preparing to spend a few weeks away from Washington for the purpose of hastening convalescence.

Edward H. Cunningham

This is in answer to an invitation extended him to appear before our Committee. I also have a letter from George Harrison, Deputy Governor of the Federal Reserve Bank of New York.

My dear Mr. Congressman:

Governor Strong sailed for Europe last week. He has not been at all well since the first of the year, and, while he did appear before your Committee last March, it was only shortly after that that he suffered a very severe attack of shingles, which has sorely racked his nerves.

George L. Harrison,
May 19, 1928

I also desire to place in the record a statement in the New York Journal of Commerce, dated May 22, 1928, from Washington.

'It is stated in well-informed circles here that the chief topic being taken up by Governor Strong of the Federal Reserve Bank of New York on his present visit to Paris is the arrangement of stabilization credits for France, Rumania, and Yugoslavia. A second vital question Mr. Strong will take up is the amount of gold France is to draw from this country.' ''

Further questioning by Chairman McFadden about the strange illness of Benjamin Strong brought forth the following testimony from Governor Charles S. Hamlin of the Federal Reserve Board on May 23rd, 1928:

''All I know is that Governor Strong has been very ill, and he has gone over to Europe primarily, I understand, as a matter of health. Of course, he knows well the various offices of the European central banks and undoubtedly will call on them.''

Governor Benjamin Strong died a few weeks after his return from Europe, without appearing before the Committee. The circumstances of his death recall the death of J. P. Morgan, a few weeks after being called to testify before the Pujo Committee in 1913 at the Money Trust Hearings.

The purpose of these hearings before the House Committee on Banking and Currency in 1928 was to investigate the necessity for passing the Strong Bill, presented by Representative Strong (no relation of Benjamin the international banker), which provided that the Federal Reserve System be empowered to act to stabilize the purchasing power of the dollar. This had been one of the promises made by Carter Glass and Woodrow Wilson when they presented the Federal Reserve Act before Congress in 1913, and such a provision had actually been put in the Act by Senator Robert L. Owen, but Carter Glass' House Committee on Banking and Currency had struck it out. The traders and speculators did not want the dollar to become stable, because they would no longer be able to make a profit. The citizens of this country had been led to gamble on the stock market in the 1920s because the traders had created a nationwide condition of instability.

The Strong Bill of 1928 was defeated in Congress. These representatives of the people did not want stability. Nobody wanted the dollar to be stable except the workers and consumers, and they had no voice in the functioning of the democracy. The closest the consumer public ever got to being represented in Congress was when the labor unions, owned by New York bankers, sent Communist-trained delegates to the House and Senate in the 1930s. It is a sad comment on the development of our civic sense that the only people whom we ever allowed to use our voice were men in the service of a foreign ideology.

Commodities could find their own prices, if they were not controlled by manipulators in the exchange markets, who, by buying and selling futures, send the price of commodities up and down. The law of supply and demand does not function in the prices of commodities, as Senator Elmer Thomas pointed out in 1938.

The financial situation in the United States during the 1920s was characterized by an inflation of speculative values only. It was purely a trader-made situation. Prices of commodities remained fairly low, despite the incredible over-pricing of securities on the exchange, far past the point where they could possibly earn a return. The purchasers did not expect their securities to return dividends. The whole idea was that they would hold them awhile and sell them at a profit. It had to stop somewhere, as Paul Warburg remarked in March, 1929, hoping to start the Crash. However, Wall Street did not let it stop until the people had put all their savings into these over-priced securities. We had the sad spectacle of the President of the United States, Calvin Collidge, acting as a shill or a come-on man for the stock market operators when he recommended to the American people that they continue buying on the market, in 1927. There had been some uneasiness about the inflated condition of the market, and the bankers showed their power by getting the President of the United States, the Secretary of the Treasury, and the Chairman of the Board of Governors of the Federal Reserve System to issue statements that brokers' loans were not too high, and that the condition of the stock market was absolutely sound.

Irving Fisher warned us in 1927 that the burden of stabilizing prices all over the world would soon fall on the United States. One of the principal results of the Second World War was the establishment of an International Monetary Fund to do just that. Professor Gustav Cassel remarked in the same year that:

"The downward movement of prices has not been a spontaneous result of forces beyond our control. It is the result of a policy deliberately framed to bring down prices and give a higher value to the monetary unit."

The Democratic Party, after passing the Federal Reserve Act and leading us into the First World War, assumed the role of a loyal opposition party during the 1920s. They were on the outside of the political fence, and were supported during those lean years by liberal handouts from Bernard Baruch, according to his biography. How far outside of it they were, and how little chance they had in 1928, is shown by a plank in the official Democratic Party platform adopted at Houston on June 28, 1928:

"The administration of the Federal Reserve System for the advantage of the stock-market speculators should cease. It must be administered for the benefit of farmers, wage-earners, merchants, manufacturers, and others engaged in constructive business."

This idealism insured defeat for its protagonist, Al Smith, who was nominated by Franklin D. Roosevelt. The campign against Al Smith also was marked by low appeals to religious intolerance, because he was a Catholic. The bankers stirred up anti-Catholic sentiment all over the country to achieve the election of their World War I protege, Herbert Hoover.

Instead of being used to promote the financial stability of the country, as had been promised by Woodrow Wilson when the Act was passed, financial instability has been steadily promoted by the Federal Reserve Board. An official memorandum issued by the Board on March 13, 1939, stated that:

"The Board of Governors of the Federal Reserve System opposes any bill which proposes a stable price level."

K. R. Bopp said before the American Economic Association in 1944 that during the 1920s, the Federal Reserve System directed open market operations not merely as a tool to make bank rate effective, but as a coequal instrument of policy "to offset the effects of gold movements." The selling out of the United States Treasury to international gold merchants occured in 1906, when Secretary of the Treasury Shaw inaugurated a gold-buying policy of advancing money to the big New York banks with which to purchase gold from abroad, so that no record of its origins need be kept by the Treasury.

Politically, the Federal Reserve Board was used to advance the election of the bankers' candidates during the 1920s. The Literary Digest on August 4, 1928, said, on the occasion of the Federal Reserve Board raising the rate to 5% in a Presidential year:

"This reverses the politically desirable cheap money policy of 1927, and gives smooth conditions on the stock market. It was attacked by the Peoples' Lobby of Washington, D. C. which said that 'This increase at a time when farmers needed cheap money to finance the harvesting of their crops was a direct blow at the farmers, who had begun to get back on their feet after the Agricultural Depression of 1920-21.' "

The New York World said on that occasion:

"Criticism of Federal Reserve Board policy by many investors is not based on its attempt to deflate the stock market, but on the charge that the Board itself, by last year's policy, is completely responsible for such stock market inflation as exists."

How the Federal Reserve Board is responsible for the stock market inflation of the 1920s and the subsequent Depression is clearly explained by Emmanuel Goldenweiser, director of research for the Board since 1920. Speaking before the American Economic Association in 1947, he said:

"Adoption in 1923 of the principle that open market operations shall be guided with a view to accomodating commerce and business and with regard to their bearing upon the general credit situation of the country was the aim of the Federal Reserve Board. It placed open market policy on the same basis as discount rate policy. One part of open market operations, however, *the purchase and liquidation by Reserve Banks of acceptances,* was left outside the control of the Open Market Committee, and even of the Federal Reserve Board. *The acceptance business was carried on as a separate activity by the Reserve Banks.*"

This was because the acceptance business was the private preserve of Paul Warburg.

Goldenweiser went on to discuss at this meeting:

"The adoption of an easy money policy in 1924, was reflected in both the reduction of discount rates and in open market purchases. It was a period when business was declining, but credit was easy and there was a movement of gold into the country. *The reasons for the policy of the Board were largely international.* It was at that time that the foundation for future credit expansion was laid, because the proceeds of the gold and the security purchases during this period were not used to reduce discounts, which were already low, but were added to member banks' reserve balances. These additional balances were largely the basis of the speculative credit expansion which occurred in the next four or five years."

Goldenweiser reveals the error of those critics of the Federal Reserve System who sought to place blame on the System for the Crash of 1929 by claiming that the Board's easy-money policy of 1927 was responsible for the stock market boom. The policy of 1927 could not have created such an enormous credit expansion. Credit had been pyramiding upon itself since 1923 and 1924, when hundreds of millions of dollars in gold were poured into this country from France and England. Goldenweiser says:

"A similar but less important program of easy money was pursued in 1927."

A more damning survey of the Federal Reserve System's first fifteen years appears in the North American Review of May, 1929, by H. Parker Willis, professional economist who was one of the authors of the Act and First Secretary of the Board from 1914 until 1920.

"My first talk with President-elect Wilson was in 1912. Our conversation related entirely to banking reform. I asked whether he felt confident we could secure the administration of a suitable law, and how we should get it applied and enforced. He answered:

'We must rely on American business idealism.' He sought for something which could be trusted to afford opportunity to American Idealism. It did serve to finance the World War and to revise American banking practices. The element of idealism that the President prescribed and believed we could get on the principle of noblesse oblige from American bankers and business men was not there. Since the inauguration of the Federal Reserve Act we have suffered one of the most serious financial depressions and revolutions ever known in our history, that of 1920-21. We have seen our agriculture pass through a long period of suffering and even of revolution, during which one million farmers left their farms, due to difficulties with the price of land and the odd status of credit conditions. We have suffered the most extensive era of bank failures ever known in this country. Forty-five hundred banks have closed their doors since the Reserve System began functioning. In some Western towns there have been times when all banks in that community failed, and given banks have failed over and over again. There has been little difference in liability to failure between members and non-member banks of the Federal Reserve System.

"Wilson's choice of the first members of the Federal Reserve Board was not especially happy. They represented a composite group chosen for the express purpose of placating this, that, or the other big interest. It was not strange that appointees used their places to pay debts. When the Board was considering a resolution to the effect that future members of the reserve system should be appointed solely on merit, because of the demonstrated incompetence of some of their number, Comptroller John Skelton Williams moved to strike out the word 'solely', and in this he was sustained by the Board. The inclusion of *certain elements* (Warburg, Strauss, etc.) in the Board gave an opportunity for catering to special interests that was to prove disastrous later on.

"President Wilson erred, as he often erred, in supposing that the holding of an important office would transform an incumbent and revivify his patriotism. The Reserve Board reached the low ebb of the Wilson period with the appointment of a member who was chosen for his ability to get delegates for a Democratic candidate for the Presidency. However, this level was not the dregs reached under President Harding. He appointed an old crony, D. R. Crissinger, as Governor of the Board, and named several other super-serviceable

politicians to other places. Before his death he had done his utmost
to debauch the whole undertaking. The System has gone steadily
downhill ever since.

"Reserve Banks had hardly assumed their first form when it
became apparent that local bankers had sought to use them as a
means of taking care of 'favorite sons', that is, persons who had by
common consent become a kind of general charge upon the banking
community, or inefficients of various kinds. When reserve directors
were to be chosen, the country bankers often refused to vote, or, when
they voted, cast their ballots as directed by city correspondents. In
these circumstances popular or democratic control of reserve banks
was out of the question. Reasonable efficiency might have been
secured if honest men, recognizing their public duty, had assumed
power. If such men existed, they did not get on the Federal Reserve
Board. In one reserve bank today the chief management is in the
hands of a man who never did a day's actual banking in his life,
while in another reserve institution both Governor and Chairman are
the former heads of now defunct banks. They naturally have a high
failure record in their district. In a majority of districts the standard
of performance as judged by good banking standards is disgracefully
low among reserve executive officials. The policy of the Federal Reserve Bank of Philadelphia is known in the System as the 'Friends
and Relatives Banks.'

"It was while making war profits in considerable amounts that
someone conceived the idea of using the profits to provide themselves with phenomenally costly buildings. Today the Reserve Banks
must keep a full billion dollars of their money constantly at work
merely to pay their own expenses in normal times.

"The best illustration of what the System has done and not
done is offered by the experience which the country was having with
speculation, in May 1929. Three years prior to that, the present bull
market was just getting under way. In the autumn of 1926 a group
of bankers, among them one of world-famous name, were sitting at a
table in a Washington hotel. One of them raised the question whether
the low discount rates of the System were not likely to encourage
secpulation.

"Yes,' replied the famous banker, 'they will, but that cannot
be helped. It is the price we must pay for helping Europe.'

"It may well be questioned whether the encouragement of
speculation by the Board has been the price paid for helping Europe
or whether it is the price paid to induce a certain class of financiers
to help Europe, but in either case European conditions should not
have had anything to do with the Board's discount policy. The fact
of the matter is that the Federal Reserve Banks do not come into
contact with the community.

"The 'small man' from Maine to Texas has gradually been led

to invest his savings in the stock market, with the result that the rising tide of speculation, transacted at a higher and higher rate of speed, has swept over the legitimate business of the country.

"In March, 1928, Roy A. Young, Governor of the Board, was called before a Senate Committee. 'Do you think the brokers' loans are too high?' he was asked.

" 'I am not prepared to say whether brokers' loans are to high or too low,' he replied, 'but I am sure they are safely and conservatively made.'

"Secretary of the Treasury Mellon in a formal statement assured the country that they were not too high, and Coolidge, using material supplied him by the Federal Reserve Board, made a plain statement to the country that they were not too high. The Federal Reserve Board, charged with the duty of protecting the interests of the average man, thus did its utmost to assure the average man that he should feel no alarm about his savings. Yet the Federal Reserve Board issued on February 2, 1929, a letter addressed to the Reserve Bank Directors cautioning them against the grave danger of further speculation.

"What could be expected from a group of men such as composed the Board, a set of men who were solely interested in standing from under when there was any danger of friction, displaying a bovine and canine appetite for credit and praise, while eager only to 'stand in' with the 'big men' whom they know as the masters of American finance and banking?"

The complete disillusionment of H. Parker Willis with the Federal Reserve System, for which he was partly responsible, demonstrates an awareness of the international influences at work on the Board of Governors, but he could not name or attack those influences.

Chapter Twelve

HERBERT HOOVER

R. G. Hawtrey, the English economist, said, in the March 1926 American Economic Review:

"When external investment outstrips the supply of general savings the investment market must carry the excess with money borrowed from the banks. A remedy is control of credit by a rise in bank rate."

The Federal Reserve Board applied this control of credit, but not in 1926, nor as a remedial measure. It was not applied until 1929, and then the rate was raised as a punitive measure, to freeze out everybody but the big trusts.

Professor Cassel, in the Quarterly Journal of Economics, August 1928, wrote that:

"The fact that a central bank fails to raise its bank rate in accordance with the actual situation of the capital market very much increases the strength of the cyclical movement of trade, with all its pernicious effects on social economy. A rational regulation of the bank rate lies in our hands, and may be accomplished only if we perceive its importance and decide to go in for such a policy. With a bank rate regulated on these lines the conditions for the development of trade cycles would be radically altered, and indeed, our familiar trade cycles would be a thing of the past. "

This is the most authoritative statement yet made on the fact that our business depressions are artificially made. The occurrence of the Panic of 1907, the Agricultural Depression of 1920, and the Great Depression of 1929, all three in good crop years and in periods of high national prosperity, should indicate a nigger in the woodpile. Lord Mayard Keynes pointed out that most theories of the business cycle failed to relate their analysis adequately to the money mechanism. Any survey or study of a depression which failed to list such factors as gold movements and pressures on foreign exchange would be worthless, yet no American economists have ever done this.

The League of Nations had achieved its goal of getting the nations of Europe back on the gold standard by 1928, but three-fourths of the world's gold was in France and the United States. The problem was how to get that gold to countries which needed it as a basis for money and credit. The answer was the Federal Reserve System.

Following the secret meeting of the Federal Reserve Board and the heads of the foreign central banks in 1927, the Federal Reserve Banks in a few months doubled their holdings of Government securities and acceptances, which resulted in the exportation of five hundred million dollars in gold in that year. The System's cheap money rate and purchases of Government securities on the open market forced the rates of call money down on the Stock Exchange, and forced gold out of the country. Foreigners also took this opportunity to purchase heavily of Government securities because of the low call money rate.

On February 6, 1929, Mr. Montagu Norman, Governor of the Bank of England, came to Washington and had a conference with Andrew Mellon, Secretary of the Treasury. Immediately after that mysterious visit, the Federal Reserve Board abruptly changed its policy and pursued a high discount rate policy, abandoning the cheap money policy which it had inaugurated in 1927 after Mr. Norman's other visit. The stock market crash and the deflation of the American people's financial structure was scheduled to take place in March. To get the ball rolling, Paul Warburg gave the official warning to the traders to get out of the market. In his annual report to the stockholders of his International Acceptance Bank, in March 1929, Mr. Warburg said:

"If the orgies of unrestained speculation are permitted to spread, the ultimate collapse is certain not only to affect the speculators themselves, but to bring about a general depression involving the entire country."

During three years of "unrestrained speculation", Mr. War burg had not seen fit to make any remarks about the condition of the Stock Exchange. A friendly organ, the New York Times, not only gave the report two columns on its editorial page, but editorially commented on the wisdom and profundity of Mr. Warburg's observations. Mr. Warburg's concern was genuine, for the stock market bubble had gone much farther than it had been intended to go, and the bankers feared the consequences if the people realized what had been done to them. When his report in the New York Times started a sudden wave of selling on the Exchange, the bankers grew panicky, and it was decided to ease the market somewhat. Accordingly, Warburg's National City Bank rushed twenty-five million dollars in cash to the call money market, and postponed the day of the crash.

The Federal Reserve Board had already warned the stockholders of the Federal Reserve Banks to get out of the Market, on February 6, 1929, but it had not bothered to say anything to the rest of the people. Nobody knew what was going on except the Wall Street bankers who were running the show. Gold movements, which would have given the situation away, were carried on with almost complete secrecy, and official reports of such movements were completely unreliable. The Quarterly Journal of Economics noted that:

"The question has been raised, not only in this country, but in several European countries, as to whether customs statistics record with accuracy the movements of the precious metals, and, when investigation has been made, confidence in such figures has been weakened rather than strengthened. Any movement between France and England, for instance, should be recorded in each country, but such comparison shows an average yearly discrepancy of fifty million francs for France and eighty-five million francs for England. These enormous discrepancies are not accounted for."

The Right Honorable Reginald McKenna stated that:

"Study of the relations between changes in gold stock and movement in price levels shows what should be very obvious, but is by no means recognized, that the gold standard is in no sense automatic in operation. The gold standard can be, and is, usefully managed and controlled for the benefit of a small group of international traders."

In August 1929, the Federal Reserve Board raised the rate to 6 percent. The Bank of England in the next month raised its rate from 5 1-2 percent to 6 1-2 percent. Dr. Friday in the September, 1929, issue of Review of Reviews, can find no reason for the Board's action:

"The Federal Reserve statement for August 7, 1929, shows that signs of inadequacy for autumn requirements do not exist. Gold resources are considerably more than the previous year, and gold continues to move in, to the financial embarrassment of Germany and England. The reasons for the Board's action must be sought elsewhere. The public has been given only the hint that 'The problem has presented difficulties because of certain peculiar conditions.' Every reason which Governor Young advanced for lowering the bank rate last year exists now. Increasing the rate means that not only is there danger of drawing gold from abroad, but imports of the yellow metal have been in progress for the last four months. To do anything to accentuate this is to take the responsibility for bringing on a world-wide credit deflation."

Thus we find that not only was the Federal Reserve System responsible for the First World War, which it made possible by enabling the United States to finance the Allies, but its policies brought on the world-wide depression of 1929-31. Governor Adolph C. Miller stated at the Senate Investigation of the Federal Reserve Board in 1931 that:

"If we had had no Federal Reserve System, I do not think we would have had as bad a speculative situation as we had, to begin with."

Carter Glass replied, "You have made it clear that the Federal Reserve Board provided a terrific credit expansion by these open market transactions."

Emmanuel Goldenweiser said: "In 1928-29 the Federal Reserve Board was engaged in an attempt to restrain the rapid increase in security loans and in stock market speculation. The continuity of this policy of restraint, however, was interrupted by reductions in bill rates in the autumn of 1928 and the summer of 1929."

Both J. P. Morgan and Kuhn, Loeb Co. had "preferred lists" of men to whom they sent advance announcements of profitable stocks. The men on these preferred lists were allowed to purchase these stocks at cost, that is, anywhere from 2 to 15 points a share less than they were sold to the public. The men on these lists were fellow bankers, prominent industrialists, powerful city politicians, national Committeemen of the Republican and Democratic Parties, and rulers of foreign countries. The men on these lists were notified of the coming crash, and sold all but so-called gilt-edged stocks, General Motors, Dupont, etc. The prices on these stocks also sank to record lows, but they came up soon afterwards. How the big bankers operated in 1929 is revealed by a Newsweek story on May 30, 1936, when a Roosevelt appointee, Ralph W. Morrison, resigned from the Federal Reserve Board:

"The consensus of opinion is that the Federal Reserve Board has lost an able man. He sold his Texas utilities stock to Insull for ten million dollars, and in 1929 called a meeting and ordered his banks to close out all security loans by September 1. As a result, they rode through the depression with flying colors."

Amazingly enough, all of the big bankers rode through the depression "with flying colors." The people who suffered were the workers and farmers who had invested their money in get-rich stocks, after the President of the United States, Calvin Coolidge, and the Secretary of the Treasury, Andrew Mellon, had persuaded them to do it.

There had been some warnings of the approaching crash in England, which American newspapers never saw. The London Statist on May 25, 1929 said:

"The banking authorities in the United States apparently want a business panic to curb speculation."

The London Economist on May 11, 1929, said:

"The events of the past year have seen the beginnings of a new technique, which, if maintained and developed, may succeed in 'rationing the speculator without injuring the trader.' "

Governor Charles S. Hamlin quoted this statement at the Senate Hearings in 1931 and said, in corroboration of it:

"That was the feeling of certain members of the Board, to remove Federal Reserve credit from the speculator without injuring the trader."

Governor Hamlin did not bother to point out that the "speculators" he was out to break were the school-teachers and small town merchants who had put their savings into the stock market, or that the "traders" he was trying to protect were the big Wall Street operators, Bernard Baruch and Paul Warburg.

When the Federal Reserve Bank of New York raised its rate to 6 percent on August 9, 1929, the market conditions began which culminated in the tremendous selling orders from October 24 into November, which wiped out a hundred and sixty billion dollars worth of security values. That was a hundred and sixty billions which the American citizens had one month and did not have the next. Some idea of the calamity may be had if we remember that our enormous outlay of money and goods in the Second World War amounted to not much more than two hundred billions of dollars, and a great deal of that remained as negotiable securities in the national debt. The stock market crash is the greatest misfortune which the United States has ever suffered.

The Academy of Political Science of Columbia University in its annual meeting on January 1930, held a post-mortem on the Crash of 1929. Vice-President Paul Warburg was to have presided, and Director Ogden Mills was to have played an important part in the discussion. However, these two gentlemen did not show up. Professor Oliver M. W. Sprague of Harvard University remarked of the crash:

"We have here a beautiful laboratory case of the stock market's dropping apparently from its own weight." It was pointed out that there was no exhaustion of credit, as in 1893, nor any currency famine, as in the Panic of 1907, when clearing-house certificates were resorted to, nor a collapse of commodity prices, as in 1920. Nor were there any bank crashes. What then, had caused the crash? The people had purchased stocks at high prices and expected the prices to continue to rise. The prices had to come down, and they did. It was obvious to the economists and bankers gathered over their brandy and cigars at the Hotel Astor that the people were at fault. Certainly the people had made a mistake in buying over-priced securities, but they had been talked into it by every leading citizen from the President of the United States on down. Every magazine of national circulation, every big newspaper, and every prominent banker, economist, and politician, had joined in the big confidence game of getting people to buy those over-priced securities. When the Federal Reserve Bank of New York raised its rate to 6 percent, in August 1929, people began to get out of the market, and it turned into a panic which drove the prices of securities down far below their natural levels. As in previous panics, this enabled both Wall Street and foreign operators in the know to pick up "blue-chip" and "gilt-edged" securities for a fraction of their real value.

The Crash of 1929 also saw the formation of giant holding companies which picked up these cheap bonds and securities, such as the Marine Midland Corporation, the Lehman Corporation, and the Equity Corporation. In 1929 J. P. Morgan Company organized the giant food trust, Standard Brands. It was an unequalled opportunity for trust operators to enlarge and consolidate their holdings.

Emmanuel Goldenweiser, director of research for the Federal Reserve System, said, in 1947:

"It is clear in retrospect that the Board should have ignored the speculative expansion and allowed it to collapse of its own weight." This admission of error eighteen years after the event was small comfort to the people who lost their savings in the Crash.

The Wall Street Crash of 1929 was the beginning of a world-wide credit deflation which lasted through 1932, and from which the Western democracies did not recover until they began to rearm for the Second World War. During this depression the trust operators achieved further control by their backing of three international swindlers, the Van Sweringen brothers, Samuel Insull, and Ivar Kreuger. These men pyramided billions of dollars worth of securities up on each other to fantastic heights. The bankers who promoted them and floated their stock issues could have broken them at any time by calling loans of less than a million dollars, but they let these men go on until they had incorporated many industrial and financial properties into holding companies, which the banks then took over for nothing. Insull piled up public utility holdings throughout the Middle West, which the banks got for a fraction of their worth. Ivar Kreuger was backed by Lee Higginson Company, supposedly one of the nation's most reputable banking houses. The Saturday Evening Post called him "more than a financial titan", and the English Review Fortnightly said, in an article written December 1931, under the title, "A Chapter in Constructive Finance": "It is as a financial irrigator that Kreuger has become of such vital importance to Europe."

"Financial irrigator", we may remember, was the title bestowed upon Jacob Schiff by Newsweek Magazine, when it described how Schiff had bought up American railroads with Rothschild's money.

The New Republic remarked on January 25th, 1933, when it commented on the fact that Lee Higginson Company had handled Kreuger and Toll securities on the American market:

"Three-quarters of a billion dollars was made away with. Who was able to dictate to the French police to keep secret the news of this extremely important *suicide* for some hours, during which somebody sold Kreuger securities in large amounts, thus getting out of the market before the debacle?"

The Federal Reserve Board could have checked the enormous credit expansion of Insull and Kreuger by investigating the security on which their loans were being made, but the Governors never made any reference to the activites of these men.

The modern bank, with the credit facilities it affords, gives an opportunity which had not previously existed for such operators as Kreuger to make an appearance of abundant capital by the aid of borrowed capital. This enables the speculator to buy securities with securities. The only limit to the amount he can corner is the amount to which the banks will back him, and, if a speculator is being promoted by a reputable banking house, as Kreuger was promoted by Lee Higginson Company, the only way he could be stopped would be by an investigation of his actual financial resources, which in Kreuger's case, proved to be nil.

The leader of the American people during the Crash of 1929 and the subsequent depression was Herbert Hoover. After the first break of the market (the five billion dollars in security values which disappeared on October 24, 1929) President Hoover said:

"The fundamental business of the country, that is, production and distribution of commodities, is on a sound and prosperous basis." His Secretary of the Treasury, Andrew Mellon, stated on December 25, 1929, that:

"The Government's business is in sound condition." His own business, the Aluminum Company of America, apparently was not doing so well, for he reduced the wages of all employees by ten per cent. This may not have been an index to the status-of the company's financial condition. Very likely, it was only an economy measure.

Chapter Thirteen
FRANKLIN D. ROOSEVELT

The Federal Reserve Bank of New York dropped its rate from 6 percent on November 1, 1929 to 1 1-2 percent on May 8, 1931. Evidently the big operators had bought all they wanted.

In 1930 Herbert Hoover appointed to the Federal Reserve Board an old friend from World War I days, Eugene Meyer, Jr., who had a long record of public service dating from 1915, when he went into partnership with Bernard Baruch in the Alaska-Juneau Gold Mining Company. Meyer had been a Special Advisor to the War Industries Board on Non-Ferrous Metals (gold, silver, etc.); Special Assistant to the Secretary of War on aircraft production; in 1917 he was appointed to the National Committee on War Savings, and was made Chairman of the War Finance Corporation from 1918-1926. He then was appointed chairman of the Federal Farm Loan Board from 1927-29. Hoover put him on the Federal Reserve Board in 1930, and Franklin D. Roosevelt created the Reconstruction Finance Corporation for him in 1932, and he headed the International Bank for Reconstruction and Development in 1946. Meyer must have been a man of exceptional ability to hold so many important posts. However, there were some Senators who did not believe he should hold any Government office, because of his family background as an international gold dealer and his mysterious operations in billions of dollars of Government securities in the First World War. Consequently, the Senate held Hearings to determine whether Meyer ought to be on the Federal Reserve Board.

At these Hearings, Representative Louis T. McFadden, Chairman of the House Banking and Currency Committee, said:

"Eugene Meyer, Jr. has had his own crowd with him in the government since he started in 1917. His War Finance Corporation personnel took over the Federal Farm Loan System, and almost immediately afterwards, the Kansas City Joint Stock Land Bank and the Ohio Joint Stock Land Bank failed.

REPRESENTATIVE RAINEY: Mr. Meyer, when he nominally resigned as head of the Federal Farm Loan Board, did not really cease his activities there. He left behind him an able body of wreckers. They are continuing his policies and consulting with him. Before his appointment, he was frequently in consultation with Assistant Secretary of the Treasury Dewey. Just before his appointment, the Chicago Joint Land Stock Bank, the Dallas Joint Stock Land Bank, the Kansas City Joint Land Stock Bank, and the Des Moines Land Bank were all functioning. Their bonds were selling at par. The then farm loan commissioner had an understanding with Secretary Dewey that nothing would be done without the consent and approval of the Federal Farm Loan Board. A few days afterwards, United States Marshals, with pistols strapped at their sides, and sometimes with drawn pistols, entered these five banks and demanded that the banks be turned over to them. Word went out all over the United States, through the newspapers, as to what had happened, and these banks were ruined. This led to the breach with the old Federal Farm Loan Board, and to the resignation of three of its members, and the appointment of Mr. Meyer to be head of that board.

SENATOR CAREY: Who authorized the marshals to take over the banks?

REP. RAINEY: Assistant Secretary of the Treasury Dewey. That started the ruin of all these rural banks, and the Gianninis bought them up in great numbers.''

World's Work of April, 1931, says:

''Ninety per cent of all the bank failures occurred in towns of less than ten thousand population. Our rural communities have had too many banks, which were inadequately capitalized to withstand the strain of postwar adjustments. We need fewer banks and more regulations. The Federal Reserve System itself rests upon bedrock, but in the field of local credit we need real banking brains.''

Rural banks could scarcely be expected to withstand such commitments as the international dealings of Wall Street.

World's Work of February 1931, said:

''When the World War began for us in 1917, Mr. Eugene Meyer, Jr. was among the first to be called to Washington. In April, 1918, President Wilson named him Director of the War Finance Corporation. This corporation loaned out 700 million dollars to banking and financial institutions.''

The Senate Hearings on Eugene Meyer, Jr. continued:

REPRESENTATIVE MCFADDEN: ''Lazard Freres, the international banking house of New York and Paris, was a Meyer family banking house. It frequently figures in imports and exports of gold, and one of the important functions of the Federal Reserve System has to do with gold movements in the maintenance of its own operations. In looking over the minutes of the hearing we had last Thursday, Senator Fletcher had asked Mr. Meyer, 'Have you any connections with international banking?' Mr. Meyer had answered, 'Me? Not personally.' This last question and answer do not appear in the stenographic transcript. Senator Fletcher remembers asking the question, and the answer. It is an odd omission.

SENATOR BROOKHART: I understand that Mr. Meyer looked it over for corrections.

REP. MCFADDEN: Mr. Meyer is a brother-in-law of George Blumenthal, a member of the firm of J. P. Morgan Company, which represents the Rothschild interests. He also is a liason officer between the French Government and J. P. Morgan. Edmund Platt, who had eight years to go on a term of ten years as Governor of the Federal Reserve Board, resigned to make room for Mr. Meyer. Platt was given a Vice-Presidency of Marine Midland Corporation by Meyer's brother-in-law Alfred A. Cook. Eugene Meyer, Jr. as head of the War Finance Corporation, engaged in the placing of two billion dollars in Government securities, placed many of those orders first with the banking house now located at 14 Wall Street in the name of Eugene Meyer, Jr. Mr. Meyer is now a large stockholder in the Allied Chemical Corporation. I call your attention to House Report No. 1635, 68th Congress, 2nd Session, which reveals that *at least twenty-four million dollars in bonds were duplicated. Ten billion dollars worth of bonds were surreptitiously destroyed.* Our committee on Banking and Currency found the records of the War Finance Corporation under Eugene Meyer, Jr. extremely faulty. While the books were being brought before our committee by the people who were custodians of them and taken back to the Treasury at night, the committee discovered that alterations were being made in the permanent records.''

This record of public service did not prevent Eugene Meyer, Jr. from continuing to serve the American people on the Federal Reserve Board, as Chairman of the Reconstruction Finance Corporation, and as head of the International Bank.

President Rand, of the Marine Midland Corporation, questioned about his sudden desire for the services of Edmund Platt, said:

"We pay Mr. Platt $22,000 a year, and we took his secretary over, of course.'' This meant another five thousand a year.

Senator Brookhart showed that Eugene Meyer, Jr. administered the Federal Farm Loan Board against the interests of the American farmer, saying:

"Mr. Meyer never loaned more than 180 million dollars of the capital stock of 500 million dollars of the farm loan board, so that in aiding the farmers he was not even able to use half of the capital.

MR. MEYER: Senator Kenyon wrote me a letter which showed that I cooperated with great advantage to the people of Iowa.

SENATOR BROOKHART: You went out and took the opposite side from the Wall Street crowd. They always send somebody out to do that. I have not yet discovered in your statements much interest in making loans to the farmers at large, or any real effort to help their condition. In your two years as head of the Federal farm loan board you made very few loans compared to your capital. You loaned only one-eighth of the demand, according to your own statement.''

Despite the damning evidence uncovered at these Senate Hearings, Eugene Meyer, Jr. remained on the Federal Reserve Board.

In 1932, the American people elected Franklin D. Roosevelt President of the United States. This was hailed as the freeing of the American people from the evil influence which had brought on the Great Depression, the ending of Wall Street domination, and the disappearance of the banker from Washington.

One of the men Roosevelt brought down from New York with him as a Special Advisor to the Treasury was Earl Bailie of J. & W. Seligman Company, who had become notorious as the man who handed the $415,000 bribe to Juan Leguia, son of the President of Peru, in order to get the President to accept a loan from J. & W. Seligman Company. There was a great deal of criticism of this appointment, and Mr. Roosevelt, in keeping with his new role as defender of the people, sent Earl Bailie back to bribing in New York.

Franklin D. Roosevelt himself was an international banker of ill repute, having floated large issues of foreign bonds in this country in the 1920s. These bonds defaulted, and our citizens lost millions of dollars, but they still wanted Mr. Roosevelt as President. The New York Directory of Directors lists Mr. Roosevelt as President and Director of United European Investors, Ltd., in 1923 and 1924, which floated many millions of German marks in this country, all of which defaulted. Poor's Directory of Directors lists him as a Director of The International Germanic Trust Company in 1928. Franklin D. Roosevelt was also an advisor to the Federal International Banking Corporation, an Anglo-American outfit dealing in foreign securities in the United States.

Roosevelt's law firm of Roosevelt and O'Connor during the 1920s represented many international banking corporations. His law partner, Basil O'Connor, was a Director in the Following corporations:

Cuban-American Manganese Corporation, Venezuela-Mexican Oil Corporation, Honduras Timber Corporation, Federal International Corporation, West Indies Sugar Corporation, American Reserve Insurance Corporation, Warm Springs Foundation. He was Director in other corporations, and later head of the American Red Cross.

When Franklin D. Roosevelt took office as President of the United States, he appointed as Director of the Budget James Paul Warburg, son of Paul Warburg, and Vice President of the Internation Acceptance Bank and other corporations. Roosevelt appointed as Secretary of the Treasury W. H. Woodin, one of the biggest industrialists in the country, Director of the American Car and Foundry Company and numerous other locomotive works, Remington Arms, The Cuba Company, Consolidated Cuba Railroads, and other big corporations. Woodin was later replaced by Henry Morgenthau, Jr., son of the Harlem real estate operator who had helped put Woodrow Wilson in the White House. With such a crew as this, Roosevelt's promises of radical social changes showed little likelihood of fulfillment. One of the first things he did was to declare a bankers' moratorium, to help the bankers get their records in order.

World's Work says:

"Congress has left Charles G. Dawes and Eugene Meyer, Jr. free to appraise, *by their own methods*, the security which prospective borrowers of the two billion dollar capital may offer."

Roosevelt also set up the Securities Exchange Commission, to see to it that no new faces got into the Wall Street gang, which caused the following colloquy in Congress:

REPRESENTATIVE WOLCOTT: At hearings before this committee in 1933, the economists showed us charts which proved beyond all doubt that the dollar value of commodities followed the price level of gold. It did not, did it?

LEON HENDERSON: No.

REPRESENTATIVE GIFFORD: Wasn't Joe Kennedy put in by President Roosevelt because he was sympathetic with big business?

LEON HENDERSON: I think so.

Paul Einzig pointed out in 1935 that:

"President Roosevelt was the first to declare himself openly in favor of a monetary policy aiming at a deliberately engineered rise in prices. In a negative sense his policy was successful. Between 1933 and 1935 he succeeded in reducing private indebtedness, but this was done at the cost of increasing public indebtedness." In other words, he eased the burden of debts off of the rich onto the poor, since the rich are few and the poor many.

On December 13, 1932, Louis T. McFadden, Chairman of the House Banking and Currency Committee, made a motion in the House of Representatives proposing impeachment of President Herbert Hoover. Only five men stood with him on this, and the resolution was thrown out. The Republican majority leader of the House said," Louis T. McFadden is now politically dead."

McFadden came back on May 23, 1933, to present on the floor of the House Articles of Impeachment against the Secretary of the Treasury, two Assistant Secretaries of the Treasury, the Federal Reserve Board of Governors, and the officers and directors of the Federal Reserve Banks for guilt in collusion in causing the Great Depression of 1929-31. The Articles of Impeachment were overwhelmingly defeated, and in the next Congressional elections, McFadden was defeated by thousands of dollars poured into his home district of Canton, Pennsylvania. His fellow-Congressmen started a whispering campaign that McFadden was losing his mind, and certainly any Congressman must have lost his mind to stand up on the floor of Congress and speak against the international operators.

Senator Robert L. Owen, testifying before the House Committee on Banking and Currency in 1938, said:

"I wrote into the bill which was introduced by me in the Senate on June 26, 1913, a provision that the powers of the System should be employed to promote a stable price level, which meant a dollar of stable purchasing, debt-paying power. It was stricken out. The powerful money interests got control of the Federal Reserve Board through Mr. Paul Warburg; Mr. Albert Strauss, and Mr. Adolph C. Miller, and they were able to have that secret meeting of May 18, 1920, and bring about a contraction of credit so violent it threw five million people out of employment. In 1920 that Reserve Board deliberately caused the Panic of 1921. The same people, unrestrained in the stock market, expanding credit to a great excess between 1926 and 1929, raised the price of stocks to a fantastic point where they could not possibly earn dividends, and when the people realized this, they tried to get out, resulting in the Crash of October 24, 1929.''

Senator Owen did not go into the question of whether the Federal Reserve Board could be held responsible to the public. Actually, they cannot. They are public officials who are appointed by the President, but their salaries are paid by the private stockholders of the Federal Reserve Banks. Obviously, their loyalty is to the people who pay their salaries, and so their history of criminal conspiracies against the American people since 1913 is no different from the history of Imperial Chemicals, I. G. Farben, or any other big corporation acting against the interests of the public.

Governor W .P. G. Harding of the Federal Reserve Board testified in 1921 that:

''The Federal Reserve Bank is an institution owned by the stockholding member banks. The Government has not a dollar's worth of stock in it.''

However, the Government does give the Federal Reserve System the use of its billions of dollars of credit, and this gives the Federal Reserve its characteristic of a central bank, the power to issue currency on the Government's credit. We do not have Federal Government notes or gold certificates as currency. We have Federal Reserve Bank notes, issued by the Federal Reserve Banks, and every dollar they print is a dollar in their pocket.

W. Randolph Burgess, of the Federal Reserve Bank of New York, stated before the Academy of Political Science in 1930 that:

''In its major principles of operation the Federal Reserve System is no different from other banks of issue, such as the Bank of England, the Bank of France, or the Reichsbank.''

All of these central banks have the power of issuing currency in their respective countries. Thus, the people do not own their own money in Europe, nor do they own it here. It is privately printed for private profit. The people have no sovereignty over their money, and it has developed that they have no sovereignty over other major political issues such as foreign policy.

As a central bank of issue, the Federal Reserve System had

behind it all the enormous wealth of the American people. When it began operations in 1913, it created a serious threat to the central banks of the impoverished countries of Europe. Because it represented this great wealth, it attracted far more gold than was desirable in the 1920s, and it was apparent that soon all of the world's gold would be piled up in this country. This would make the gold standard a joke in Europe, because they would have no gold over there to back their issue of money and credit. It was the Federal Reserve's avowed aim in 1927, after the secret meeting with the heads of the foreign central banks, to get large quantities of that gold sent back to Europe, and its methods of doing so, the low interest rate and heavy purchases of Government securities, which created vast sums of new money, intensified the stock market speculation and made the stock market crash and resultant depression so great a national disaster.

Since the Federal Reserve System was guilty of causing this disaster, and knew that it was guilty, we might suppose that they would have tried to alleviate it by some method. However, through the dark years of 1931 and 1932, the Governors of the Federal Reserve Board saw the plight of the American people steadily worsening, and did nothing to help them. This was more criminal than the original plotting of the Depression. Anyone who lived through those years in this country remembers the widespread unemployment, the misery, and the hunger of our people. At any time during those years the Federal Reserve Board could have acted to relieve this situation.

The problem was to get some money back into circulation. So much of the money normally used to pay rent and food bills had been sucked into Wall Street that there was no money to carry on the business of living. In many areas, people printed their own money on wood and paper, for use in their communities, and this money was good, since it represented obligations to each other which people fulfilled.

The Federal Reserve System was a central bank of issue. It had the power to, and did, when it suited its owners, issue millions of dollars of money. Why did it not do so in 1931 and 1932? The Wall Street bankers were through with Mr. Herbert Hoover, and they wanted Franklin D. Roosevelt to come in on a wave of glory as the saviour of the nation. Therefore, the American people had to starve and suffer until March of 1933, when the White Knight came riding in with his crew of Wall Street bribers and put some money into circulation. That was all there was to it. As soon as Mr. Roosevelt took office, the Federal Reserve began to buy Government securities at the rate of ten million dollars a week for ten weeks, and created a hundred million dollars in new money, which alleviated the critical famine of money and credit, and the factories started hiring people again.

Besides Roosevelt's manipulations of the price of silver for the benefit of the English family Sassoon, which brought widespread misery in China and India, he is famous for his gold operations with his Secretary of the Treasury, Henry Morgenthau, Jr. The Gold Trading Act which he rammed through Congress allowed the Secretary of the Treasury to purchase gold anywhere without any notification or authorization from any government body.

Section 8 of the Federal Reserve (Gold) Act of 1934 provided that:

'With the approval of the President, the Secretary of the Treasury may purchase gold in any amount at home or abroad, with any direct obligations, coin or currency of the United States authorized by law.''

Roosevelt's international gold dealings were put to the test of the Supreme Court. This body, it will be remembered, decided in favor of E. H. Harriman and Otto Kahn in 1908, when it ruled that these men did not have to show the records of their stock manipulations to the Interstate Commerce Commissions. This was in connection with Kuhn, Loeb's seizure of the Union Pacific Railroad. The Supreme Court has consistently acted in the interests of the money power, and Mr. Justice Owen Roberts is a Director of the Morgan outfit, American Telephone and Telegraph Corporation. Until 1919, only 33 statutes of the United States had been held unconstitutional, but 223 state statutes were voided by the Supreme Court, which has acted towards centralization of power for the past fifty years.

How Roosevelt and Morgenthau plunged into international gold manipulations is told by Alsop and Kintner, Washington columnists, in the Saturday Evening Post of April 15, 1939:

"The first thing Morgenthau did was to fire Dean Acheson of J. P. Morgan Company, then Undersecretary of the Treasury, because Acheson disagreed with some of his policies. By the Gold Reserve Act of 1934, Roosevelt and Morgenthau made paper profit of two billion, eight hundred million dollars, by valuing all the gold at $35 instead of $20.67 an ounce. Still under authority of the Gold Reserve Act, they used this fund in buying and selling gold to manage the dollar price on the world exchange. Thus they gained control of money. (The brains behind this was Bernard Baruch.) Morgenthau had been a farmer, but showed acute perception of money operations. H. Merle Cochran and Dr. Herbert Feis are two men through whom the Treasury keeps its finger on the pulse of money throughout the world. Once a month, Cochran goes to Bern, Switzerland, to hobnob with the heads of and hear the news from the European Central Banks at the meeting of the Bank for International Settlements, which is called "their club". Pearl Buck's former husband, J. Lessing Buck, who is a professor in a Chinese-American university, thus conceals his real purpose in China, his work for Morgenthau. The Chinese and American Treasuries co-operate closely, and a direct liason is necessary. Butteworth does a job like Cochran in London. Cochran officially is merely a secretary to the Embassy in Paris. Actually, he is the number-one dollar man of Europe who secretly played America's hand in the great money-game. In this absorbing international drama, you may see how world politics really work. The actors are the leading men of the United States, France, and England, their principal financial officials, their most eminent bankers, and financiers. T. K. Bewley does a like job for England at the British Embassy in Washington, and *Harry Dexter White*, special adviser on silver to the United States Treasury, cooperated closely with him. The President himself calls the transfer of the financial capital from New York to Washington one of the two great achievements of the New Deal."

Roosevelt's gold manipulations came before the Supreme Court in 1934 when Litigant F. E. Nortz sought damages from the United States, on the grounds that he had lost $65,000 on $106,000 of gold certificates which he redeemed at the United States Treasury after Roosevelt had changed the value of gold from $20.67 to $35 an ounce. The Supreme Court was placed in the difficult position of approving Roosevelt's action without betraying its sympathies for him. It had acted increasingly on behalf of the executive branch of the Government, as do all appointive officials, but it had to proceed cautiously in this instance. Newsweek Magazine of Feburay 9, 1935, says:

"The Supreme Court still debates on the gold clauses in the Banking Act of 1935. Morgenthau was preparing legislation to rush through Congress should the decision be against the administration. The Chief Clerk posted a notice that they should not reach a decision by the following Monday. Never before in its history had the Supreme Court issued an announcement of its future action."

On February 16, 1935, Newsweek observed:

"For the second time, the court posted an announcement that no decision would be reached, thus breaking precedent two weeks in a row. Two days before, the Supreme Court justices had dined with Roosevelt at the White House."

This dinner with Roosevelt during the discussion of highly controversial legislation of course had nothing to do with the Court's final decision.

Newsweek, February 23, 1935, said:

"In a 5—4 decision, the Supreme Court upheld Roosevelt, but partially rebuked Congress. It supported Congress' power to regulate the currency, and change the gold content of the dollar, and invalidate gold clauses in non-government bonds, but held that Congress was without power to reduce debt by repudiation of contract, and judged cancellation of gold clauses in government bonds illegal.

Reviewing Congress' gold laws, Chief Justice Hughes declared, 'We are not concerned with their wisdom. The question before the Court is one of power, not of policy.' Justice McReynolds, speaking for the minority in a loud and bitter tone, said:

'The Constitution, as we have known it, is gone. This is Nero at his worst. It seems impossible to overestimate what has been done here today. The guarantees which men and women heretofore have looked to to protect their interests have all been swept away. There are some responsibilities attaching to a man on this bench, to reveal to the bar, in all its nakedness, just what has been done. We are confronted with a condition in which the dollar may be reduced to 50c today, 30c tomorrow, 10c the next day. Loss of reputation for honorable dealing will leave us ruined. The impending legal and moral chaos is appalling.' "

It took Justice McReynolds twenty-one years to find out that the Constitution was gone. The American people do not know it yet. McReynolds' speech, to have the element of timeliness, should have been uttered on December 23, 1913, when Woodrow Wilson signed the Federal Reserve Act. This Act took away from Congress the right of monetary issue and gave it to private bankers who owned the Federal Reserve System.

"The administration had already *guessed* a decision was to come. Secretary Morgenthau was lunching with Roosevelt at the White House. Mrs. Morgenthau and Mrs. Dorn, wife of the Secretary of War, were in the Court before any of the Justices' wives."

Newsweek further remarked:

"News of the Supreme Court decision sent prices of securities and commodities rocketing. Foreign currencies spurted upwards. Jubilant over the decision, Roosevelt held back proposed National Recovery Act legislation for two days, so the Administration's victory would have no competition on the front pages. Litigant Nortz who had lost $65,000 on gold certificates, was denied damages on grounds he had not shown loss of buying power."

Chapter Fourteen
MARRINER ECCLES

The Federal Reserve Board during Roosevelt's administration underwent a complete change of personnel. Charles S. Hamlin, oldest Governor of the Board, having been appointed in 1914, and the only one of the original seven members still associated with it, stepped down in 1936 to the position of Special Counsel to the Board.

Another familiar face at the Board of Governors was Emmanuel Goldenweiser, Director of Research for the Federal Reserve Board since 1919. An immigrant from Kiev, Russia, Goldenweiser arrived in this country in 1906. He promptly entered public service, being employed in the United States Immigration Service from 1906 to 1910. From 1910 to 1914, he was employed by the Department of Agriculture, and from 1914 to 1919 by the United States Census. In 1919, he came to work for the Federal Reserve Board. As Director of Research for the Board for thirty years, he has issued many authoritative statements of policy, and undoubtedly knows more about the workings of the Federal Reserve System from the inside than any other man.

A Roosevelt appointee to the Board in 1936 was Joseph A. Broderick, an old friend from New York. Broderick had been associated with the Federal Reserve System in 1919, and from 1929 to 1934 he was State Superintendent of Banks for the State of New York. While holding this office, he was brought to trial for criminal neglect of duty in connection with the failure of the Bank of the United States. The Bank of the United States had invested heavily in New York real estate, particularly around Central Park West, and had seriously over-extended itself. As Superintendent of Banks, Broderick was aware of the condition of the Bank of the United States, but for reasons not advanced at his trial, he did nothing about it. The Bank of the United States closed its doors, and depositors lost millions of dollars. Broderick seemed likely to get a stiff jail sentence for his criminal neglect of duty, but Governor Franklin D. Roosevelt came to testify at his trial. So brilliantly did Roosevelt plead for him that Broderick not only did not go to jail, but went back, to his old job as State Superintendent of Banks. In 1936 Roosevelt appointed Broderick Governor of the Federal Reserve Board, and in 1937, Broderick resigned to accept the position of President of the East River Savings Bank, one of the oldest and biggest banks in New York City.

J. F. T. O'Connor, Comptroller of the Currency, resigned in 1933 to go to Los Angeles as a member of the McAdoo law firm. McAdoo, Secretary of the Treasury in the First World War, was now the lawyer for A .P. Giannini's giant bank-holding company, the Trans-America Corporation and the Bank of America. O'Connor was soon afterwards appointed a District Judge of California.

Other members of the Board of Governors who went on to better things were John McKee, who served from 1937 to 1946, when he was made President of the Continental Bank and Trust Company, and Chester C. Davis, who served on the Board from 1936 to 1941. Davis had been in the Agriculture Department under Henry Wallace, then went to the Commodity Credit Corporation, from there to the Export-Import Bank, and then to the Federal Reserve Board. He resigned from the Board to become President of the Federal Reserve Bank of St. Louis.

The Federal Reserve Board, insofar as the public was concerned, during the Roosevelt administration was Marriner Eccles, an emulator and admirer of the Chief. Eccles was a Utah banker, President of the First Securities Corporation, a family investment trust consisting of a number of banks which Eccles had picked up cheap during the Agricultural Depression of 1920-21. Eccles also was a director of such corporations as Pet Milk Company, Mountain States Implement Company, and Amalgamated Sugar. As a big banker, Eccles fitted in well with the group of powerful men who were operating Roosevelt.

There was some discussion in Congress as to whether Eccles ought to be on the Federal Reserve Board at the same time he had all of these banks in Utah, but he testified that he had very little to do with the First Securities Corporation besides being President of it, and so he was confirmed as Chairman of the Board.

Eugene Meyer, Jr. now resigned from the Board to spend more of his time lending the two billion dollar capital of the Reconstruction Finance Corporation, and determining the value of collateral by his own methods.

The Banking Act of 1935, which greatly increased Roosevelt's power over the nation's finances, was an integral part of the legislation by which he proposed to extend his absolute reign in the United States. It was not fought by the people as was the National Recovery Act, because it was not so naked an infringement of their liberties. It was, however, an important measure. First of all, it extended the terms of office of the Federal Reserve Board of Governors to fourteen years, or, three and a half times the length of a Presidential term. This meant that a President assuming office who might be hostile to the Board could not by any means appoint a majority to it who would be favorable to him. Thus, a monetary policy inaugurated before a President came into the White House would go on regardless of his wishes.

As Congressman Wright Patman has pointed out, the Amendments of 1935 stripped all power from the Officers and Directors of the 12 Federal Reserve Banks. He has remarked that now the Officers and Directors of a Federal Reserve Bank do not have any more power over our monetary system than the janitor of a building, because those 1935 Amendments placed all of the powers in the Board of Governors and in the Open Market Committees.

Congressman Patman's objections to the Open Market Committee make the point that that Committee should be composed of members of the Board of Governors only, and should not have on it Representatives of the private banks as at present. This excessive and dangerous centralization of monetary powers, while it might have been necessary to manage the extraordinary and astronomical expansion of United States public credit during the Second World War, is a real threat to peacetime economy, as the disastrous postwar inflation testifies. The question is, Who could see far enough ahead in 1935 to centralize those banking powers for such an expansion of credit in the 1940s? Henry Morgenthau, Harry Dexter White, Herbert Feis, and Jacob Viner were preparing for war finance when those Amendments were drafted, and war finance on a scale never before dreamed of.

The Banking Act of 1935 also repealed the clause of the Glass-Steagall Banking Act of 1933, which had provided that a banking house could not be on the Stock Exchange and also be involved in investment banking. This clause had been stuck in the Banking Act of 1933 as a sop to the people who were complaining that the bankers were responsible for the depression. The clause was a good one, since it prevented a banking house from lending money to a corporation which it owned. Still it is to be remembered that this clause covered up some other provisions in that Act, such as the creation of the Federal Deposit Insurance Corporation, providing insurance money to the amount of 150 million dollars, to guarantee fifteen billion dollars worth of deposits. This increased the power of the big bankers over small banks and gave them another excuse to investigate them. The Banking Act of 1933 also legislated that all earnings of the Federal Reserve Banks must by law go to the banks themselves. At last the provision in the Act that the Government share in the profits was gotten rid of. It had never been observed, and the increase in the assets of the Federal Reserve Banks from 143 million dollars in 1913 to 45 billion dollars in 1949 went entirely to the private stockholders of the banks. Thus, the one constructive provision of the Banking Act of 1933 was repealed in 1935, and also the Federal Reserve Banks were now permitted to loan directly to industry, thus competing with the member banks, who would not hope to compete with them in arranging large loans.

When the provision that banks could not be involved in investment banking and operate on the Stock Exchange was repealed in 1935, Carter Glass, originator of that provision, was asked by reporters:

"Does that mean that J. P. Morgan can go back into investment banking?"

"Well, why not?" replied Senator Glass. "There has been an outcry all over the country that the banks will not make loans. Now the Morgans can go back to underwriting."

Because that provision was unfavorable to them, the bankers had simply clamped down on making loans until it was repealed. Congress could not get away with passing any legislation which restricted them.

Newsweek of March 14, 1936, noted that:

"The Federal Reserve Board fired nine chairmen of Reserve Banks, explaining that "it intended to make the chairmanships of the Reserve Banks largely a part-time job on an honorary basis.' This was another instance of the gradual tightening up and centralization of control in the Federal Reserve System. The regional district system had never been an important factor in the administration of monetary policy, and the Board was now cutting down on all its officials outside of Washington.

The Federal Reserve Board itself had lost its independence in 1920, when both Warburg and Strauss had resigned. Warburg continued to dominate the Board, but his authority was gradually taken over by Secretary of the Treasury Mellon, particularly with regards the Board's open market operations in buying and selling Government securities. Thus, the Chairman of the Senate Committee on Banking and Currency had asked, during the Gold Reserve Hearings of 1934:

"Is it not true, Governor Young, that the Secretary of the Treasury for the past twelve years has dominated the policy of the Federal Reserve Banks and the Federal Reserve Board with respect to the purchase of United States bonds?"

Governor Young had denied this, but it had already been brought out that on both of his hurried trips to this country in 1927 and 1929 to dictate Federal Reserve policy, Governor Montagu Norman of the Bank of England had gone directly to Andrew Mellon, Secretary of the Treasury, to get him to purchase Government securities on the open market and start a movement of gold out of his country back to Europe.

The Gold Reserve Hearings had also brought in a parade of other people who had more than a passing interest in the operations of the Federal Reserve System. James Paul Warburg, just back from the London Economic Conference with Professor O. M. W. Sprague and Henry L. Stimson, came in to declare that he thought we ought to modernize the gold standard. Frank Vanderlip suggested that we do away with the Federal Reserve Board and set up a Federal Monetary Authority. This would have made no difference to the New York bankers, who would have selected the personnel anyway. And Senator Robert L. Owen, longtime critic of the System, made the following statement:

"The people did not know the Federal Reserve Banks were organized for profit-making. They were intended to stabilize the credit and currency supply of the country. That end has not been accomplished. Indeed, there has been the most *remarkable variation* in the purchasing power of money since the System went into effect. The Federal Reserve men are chosen by the big banks, through discreet little campaigns, and they naturally follow the ideals which are portrayed to them as the soundest from a financial point of view."

Benjamin Anderson, economist for the Chase National Bank of New York, said:

"At the moment, 1934, we have 900 million dollars excess reserves. In 1924, with increased reserves of 300 million, you got some three or four billion in bank expansion of credit very quickly. That extra money was put out by the Federal Reserve Banks in 1924 through buying government securities and was the cause of the rapid expansion of bank credit. The banks continued to get excess reserves because more gold came in, and because, whenever there was a slackening, the Federal Reserve people would put out some more. They held back a bit in 1926. Things firmed up a bit that year. And then in 1927 they put out less than 300 million additional reserves, set that wild stock market going, and that led us right into the smash of 1929.''

Dr. Anderson also stated that:

''The money of the Federal Reserve Banks is money they create. When they buy Government securities they create reserves. They pay for the Government securities by giving checks on themselves, and those checks come to the commercial banks and are by them deposited in the Federal Reserve Banks, and then money exists which did not exist before.

SENATOR BULKLEY: It does not increase the circulating medium at all?

ANDERSON: No.''

This is an explanation of the manner in which the Federal Reserve Banks increased their assets from 143 million dollars to 45 billion dollars in thirty-five years. They did not produce anything, they were non-productive enterprises, and yet they had this enormous profit, merely by creating money, 95 percent of it in the form of credit, which did not add to the circulating medium. It was not distributed among the people in the form of wages, nor did it increase the buying power of the farmers and workers. It was credit-money created by bankers for the use and profit of bankers, who increased their wealth by more than forty billion dollars in a few years because they got control of the Government's credit in 1913 by passing the Federal Reserve Act.

Marriner Eccles also had a lot to say about the creation of money. He considered himself quite an economist, and had been brought into the Government service by Stuart Chase and Rexford Guy Tugwell, two of Roosevelt's early brain-trusters. Eccles was the only one of that gang which came in with Roosevelt who stayed in office throughout his administration. Everybody else got disgusted with the way Roosevelt was turning America over to Wall Street, and quit, but Eccles, a banker himself, was quite pleased with the way Roosevelt was doing things. He also worshipped the great democrat, so that he had every reason, both business and personal, to continue to shout huzzas.

Before the House Banking and Currency Committee on June 24, 1941, Governor Eccles said:

''Money is created out of the *right* to issue credit-money.''

Turning over the Government's credit to private bankers in 1913 gave them unlimited opportunities to create money. The Federal

Reserve System could also destroy money in large quantities through open market operations. Eccles said, at the Silver Hearings of 1939:

"When you sell bonds on the open market, you extinguish reserves."

Extinguishing reserves means wiping out a basis for money and credit issue, or, tightening up on money and credit, a condition which is usually even more favorable to bankers than the creation of money. Calling in or destroying money gives the banker immediate and unlimited control of the financial situation, since he is the only one with money and the only one with the power to issue money in a time of money shortage. The money panics of 1873, 1893, 1907, 1920-21, and 1929-31, all were characterized by a drawing in of the circulating medium. In cold economical terms, this does not sound like such a terrible thing, but when it means that people do not have money to pay their rent or buy food, and when it means that an employer has to lay off three-fourths of his help because he cannot borrow the money to pay them, the enormous guilt of the bankers and the long record of suffering and misery for which they are responsible would indicate that no punishment is too severe for their crimes against their fellow-men.

On September 30, 1940, Governor Eccles said:

"If there were no debts in our money system, there would be no money."

This is an accurate statement about our money system. Instead of money being created by the production of the people, the annual increase in goods and services, it is created by the bankers out of the debts of the people. This is mainly because we hold on to the obsolete gold standard as the basis for the issue of money and credit. Many bankers and economists have stated that the gold standard is inadequate, and much of the poverty and hunger among the people is due to the fact that an adequate monetary system does not exist. The inadequacy of the present monetary system means huge profits for a few, and a hand-to-mouth existence for the many. Because it is inadequate, it is subject to great fluctuations and is basically unstable. These fluctuations are also a source of great profit. For that reason, the Federal Reserve Board has consistently opposed any legislation which attempts to stabilize the monetary system. Its position has been set forth definitively in Governor Eccles' letter to Senator Wagner on March 9, 1939, and the Memorandum issued by the Board on March 13, 1939.

Governor Eccles wrote that:

" . . . you are advised that the Board of Governors of the Federal Reserve System does not favor the enactment of Senate Bill No. 31, a bill to amend the Federal Reserve Act, or any other legislation of this general character."

The Memorandum of the Board stated, in its "Memorandum on Proposals to maintain prices at fixed levels":

"The Board of Governors opposes any bill which proposes a stable price level, on the grounds that prices do not depend primarily on the price or cost of money; that the Board's control over money cannot be made complete; and that steady average prices, even if obtainable by official action, would not insure lasting prosperity."

Yet William McChesney Martin, the present Chairman of the Board of Governors said before the Subcommittee on Debt Control, the Patman Committee, on March 10, 1952 that "One of the fundamental purposes of the Federal Reserve Act is to protect the value of the dollar."

Senator Flanders questioned him: Is that specifically stated in the original legislation setting up the Federal Reserve System?

"No," replied Mr. Martin, "but it is inherent in the entire legislative history and in the surrounding circumstances."

Senator Robert L. Owen has told us how it was taken out of the original legislation against his will, and that the Board of Governors has opposed such legislation. Apparently Mr. Martin does not know this.

Steady average prices, indeed, are impossible so long as we have the speculators on the stock exchange driving prices up and down in order to reap profits for themselves. Despite Governor Eccles' insistence that steady average prices would not *insure* lasting prosperity, they could do much to bring about such a condition. A man on a yearly wage of $2,500 is not made more prosperous if the price of bread increases five cents a loaf during the year.

In 1935, Eccles said before the House Committee on Banking and Currency:

"The Government controls the gold reserve, that is, the power to issue money and credit, thus largely regulating the price structure."

This is an almost direct contradiction of Eccles' statement in 1939 that prices do not depend, primarily, on the price or cost of money.

In 1935, Governor Eccles stated before the House Committee:

"The Federal Reserve Board has the power of open-market operations. Open-market operations are the most important single instrument of control over the volume and cost of credit in this country. When I say 'credit' in this connection, I mean money, because by far the largest part of money in use by the people of this country is in the form of bank credit or bank deposits. When the Federal Reserve Banks buy bills or securities in the open market, they increase the volume of the people's money and lower its cost; and when they sell in the open market they decrease the volume of money and increase its cost. Authority over these operations, which affect the welfare of the whole people, must be invested in a body representing the national interest.''

This was a plea for extension of the powers of the Federal Reserve Board in the Banking Act of 1935, which he got. His statement that the Federal Reserve Board represents the national interest is the sheerest hypocrisy. If the First World War was in the national interest, if the Agricultural Depression was in the national interest, if the Great Depression was in the national interest, then the Federal Reserve Board represents the national interest.

At the Silver Hearings held by the Senate Finance Committee in 1939, Senator Robert L. Owen said:

''When President Roosevelt came into power six years ago the outstanding currency on March 15, 1939 was $7.2 billion; then it was *contracted* by the Federal Reserve Board and only expanded by the purchase of silver certificates as to now reach the maximum of $6.7 billion. During the first year of Roosevelt's administration the Federal Reserve Board contracted the currency by two billion dollars. At present the outstanding credits of the Federal Reserve System are a billion dollars less than they were when Roosevelt came in. Under the influence and direction of the Federal Reserve System 16,000 banks have failed in 16 years through mismanagement of the System. The loss in production in the last ten years reached $200 billion in products and services which might have been enjoyed by the people under a management which had their interests at heart, and the country would be free of debt and heavy interest charges. These facts are proven by the records of the Federal Reserve Board of Governors. I make no charges against them on which they do not stand self-convicted by their own speeches and publications. The Federal Reserve System with its enormous power, with its large bureau of research, with every opportunity to know the facts and take action to help us, has not given this country any relief, and has done all it could to worsen the situation. The only consistent action of the Board has been to set itself up firmly as an obstacle to the regulation of the value of money by Congress. The manner in which the stability of our economic life has been impaired by the mismanagement of the Federal Reserve System, and the remedies therefor, have been clearly set forth in Senate Document 23 of the 76th Congress, 1st session. The members of the Board of Governors should not be bankers. The Board and the big bankers have the power to immediately end this depression by instructing the Reserve Banks to buy bonds and notes of the United States on account of the United States at the rate of $50 million a day until such non-liquid securities converted into liquid money should correct the deficit of liquid money produced by the hoarding of demand deposits.''

In 1938, Congressman Wright Patman introduced a bill to Congress, HR 7230, which provided for government ownership of the

Federal Reserve Banks. Since the banks used the government's credit, this seemed fair enough, but the bill was defeated by Congress.

Mr. Patman testified at the Hearings on this bill:

"If the market price of securities is affected in any way, the Board of Governors become very active. I insist that if their powers are used to protect the general welfare as they have been used to protect the price of Government securities, our country would be much better off. Mr. Eccles admitted to this committee in February, 1937, that the Board of Governors adopted the policy of making money dearer in order to help investors secure a better return on their investments."

During the Patman Committee Hearings on March 17, 1952, Senator Flanders said, "It has seemed to me that the most foolproof business operation in the world was that of the Federal Reserve banks when they were pegging the bond market. They were required to buy when stuff was low, and were required to sell when their product was high."

C. F. Ross said before the annual meeting of the American Economic Association in 1947:

"Bank credit deflation as encouraged by the Federal Reserve System in 1920-21, 1929-32, and 1937-38, has an important three-way adverse effect on business which is delayed by six months. First, a change in the long-term interest rate lowers the capitalization of current profits. There are two more immediate effects on business; as a result of increasing unemployment and increase in production, (decrease in money unit wage cost) nonfarm prices drop more rapidly than prices of metals and metal products. In consequence, the demand for investment collapses and about six months after the Federal Reserve Board has initiated a deflationary policy."

R. G. Hawtrey, the English economist, writes on the effect which changes in the interest rate have on wholesale inventories. Wholesale inventories in the United States average about twenty billion dollars worth of goods which are readily convertible into cash. Thus, a change in the interest rate directly affects such a volume of goods-money. Holding the goods when there is a market for them means a depreciation and storage charges, but if the interest rates go up, the goods must be moved to get cash, while, if the interest rate goes down, money becomes cheaper and the wholesaler has to hold his goods until money becomes dearer.

Late in 1936 and throughout 1937, a sudden depression swept over the United States, popularly known as the "business recession of 1936-37." Like other depressions caused by the Federal Reserve System, businessmen were at a loss to explain this one. The country was prosperous, Mr. Roosevelt had just been re-elected against negligible opposition, and yet a depression came along which wiped out a good many people who had begun to get back on their feet after the crash of 1929.

Emmanuel Goldenweiser, director of research for the Federal Reserve Board, says:

"In the summer of 1936, banks had excess reserves. The Federal Reserve Board decided to use its newly acquired power to raise reserve requirements in order to immobilize these excess reserves. The Board repeated this action in the spring of 1937, thus ushering in the serious reaction of 1937-38."

Immobilizing reserves was the equivalent to extinguishing them, insofar as the available supply of money and credit was concerned, and, as Governor Eccles had testified, extinguishing reserves meant wiping out a basis for issuing money and credit, tightening up the money market, and ushering in a business depression.

Senator Robert L. Owen testified at the Hearings on HR 7230, the bill to make the Federal Reserve banks a national property, that:

"In 1937, when the Federal Reserve Board called upon the banks to raise their reserves to twice what they had been before, there was a contraction of credit of two billion dollars."

H. B. Elliston, editor of the Washington Post, wrote in an article in the Atlantic Monthly in July, 1938 that:

"A coincidence between the use of the Federal Reserve brakes and the running down of the economy is evident in 1936-37."

Paul Einzig, in "World Finance," MacMillan's, 1938, writes that:

"In March, 1937, Roosevelt condemned the sharp rise in commodity prices which he had encouraged since 1933, and foreshadowed measures against it. This was largely responsible for the gold scare of 1937 and the 'recession' in the United States. Professor O. M. W. Sprague, former economic adviser to the Bank of England, and proponent of the Aldrich Plan from 1910 to 1912, left in 1933 to join the United States Treasury, for whom he negotiated along with James Paul Warburg and Henry L. Stimson, during the London Economic Conference. In 1934, he resigned. During his stay in Europe in 1936, both publicly and privately, Professor Sprague stated that there was likelihood of a cut in the American buying price of gold. His remarks were repeated in all the markets. It may seem strange that such importance should have been attached to the private views of a professor, who, at that time, held no official position whatsoever, although he used the Bank of England as his mailing address, and had an office placed at his disposal there. The gold scare was artificially kept alive by other gold scaremongers. Dr. L. G. Tripp of the Netherlands Bank, and President of the Bank for International Settlements, in the annual report for 1936-37, had a chapter entitled 'A Year of Mounting Gold Supplies.' Professor Cassel carried on the propaganda against gold. Roosevelt made a public statement denying that the price of gold would be reduced 'at this time', which, indicating as it did a future reduction, only made matters worse.''

The President of the United States lending his active support to further a group of international gold dealers may seem a difficult fact to some people, but this was only one incident of Roosevelt's use of his high office to help his friends.

One of the most reprehensible of the scoundrels heretofore named in this chronicle of rascality is the aforementioned Professor Oliver M. W. Sprague, who figures in this work from its first to its last pages. We find Sprague in 1904 busily writing articles insisting that we have a central bank. A Professor of Economics at Harvard in 1911, he was writing propaganda for the Aldrich Plan. In 1913, he was writing propaganda for the Federal Reserve Act, saying that it was really a bankers' benefit. In the 1920s, he was writing a series of articles defending the gold standard. In the 1930's, he was skipping about the financial capitals of the world, running errands for the international gold merchants. No wonder a mere *professor* had an office placed at his disposal in the Bank of England! This Harvard economist joined the United States Treasury for a few months and immediately was sent to represent the interests of this country at the London Economic Conference, a man who had never before worked for the Government. In 1937 he was a key member of the Economists' Committee on Monetary Policy, a lobbying organization for Wall Street which, according to its own records, spent $45,000 on literature opposing the monetary reforms of Senator Elmer Thomas, who had that year proposed a commodity dollar system.

Chapter Fifteen

HERBERT LEHMAN

The newest name in the international financial hierarchy is Herbert Lehman. Of 106 firms which founded the New York Cotton Exchange in 1870, only two survived to 1940, Lehman Brothers and Hentz and Company. Hentz and Company was taken over by the Baruch Brothers in 1917 when it became inadvisable to continue the firm of Baruch Brothers, bankers, since Bernard Baruch was entering public service. Anna Rochester wrote in 1935 that the banking leadership of Kuhn, Loeb Co. was being replaced by the more progressive methods of Lehman Brothers. 1935 was the year of the Nye Committee investigation of profiteers and munitions-makers in the First World War. The DuPonts were made the scapegoats of that investigation, the purpose being to frighten Congress into accepting without amendment all of Baruch's plans for controlling this country during the Second World War. In a series of lectures to the Nye Committee, he outlined, step by step, the draft, rationing of food and essential wartime materials such as oil and rubber, in which he had large interests, the cost-plus manufacturing system, price control, and the corporate excess profits tax system. The Baruch plans were followed minutely in setting up the military dictatorship which ruled this country from 1940 to 1945.

Chairman Lister Hill of the Nye Committee stated on January 28, 1937, that:

"We are very fortunate in having with us this morning as our witness Mr. Bernard Baruch. As you gentlemen will recall, Mr. Baruch was the Chairman of the War Industries Board set up by Woodrow Wilson during the First World War. It can be said without exaggeration that there is no man in the country who has given more time, more thought, to the subject of taking the profits out of war than Mr. Baruch."

Whether Chairman Hill was being witty, we cannot say, but certainly Mr. Baruch had taken as many profits out of war as anybody in this country. As mentioned earlier, Baruch had profited by a phony peace rumor in 1918 which netted him a profit of $750,000 in one day on stock in United States Steel. In 1935, at the Nye Committee Hearings, Mr. Baruch had testified that:

"All wars are economic in their origin."

Other interesting statements of Mr. Baruch are given in the following extracts from the Committee Hearings

"If the Germans had been smart enough, we could not have won that war. There was 35 percent of the nitrates we could not get. There was a great battle between the two economic sysems as to which would get the product. We had the gold which we would promise the Chilean government. We promised that we would give them the gold within six months after the signing of the treaty of peace. We earmarked the gold in our Treasury for them on the condition that they would do certain things. We were able in that way to get what we wanted in the way of nitrates.

MR. FADDIS: Do you think section 5 of your proposal is broad enough to include control of the conscientious objectors we would have in time of war? There is a group which seems to be growing a great deal.

MR. BARUCH: Your draft act would have to take care of that. That is one of the things you would have to set up.

MR. COSTELLO: The thought I had was the possibility of the conscientious objector being *compelled* to take part in some useful occupation.

MR. BARUCH: *He works or fights.* We will put him in something that is useful."

In 1935, here were the representatives of the people of the United States calmly discussing the dictatorship they were going to set up over their own people. Again Mr. Baruch at the Nye Committee hearings:

MR. BARUCH: "The President (Wilson) one time gave me a letter authorizing me to take over any industry or plant. There was Judge Gary, President of United States Steel, whom we were having trouble with, and when I showed that to him, he said, 'I guess we will have to fix this up', and he did fix it up. You gentlemen will have your ceiling on prices to start with, and you can commandeer any plant during the war."

Miss Jeanette Rankin commented, during the Nye Hearings, that: 'It is perfectly possible to take the profits out of war, but it is not possible to take the profits out of war by any of the schemes that you rich men suggest, and you haven't had any proposals for taking the profits out of war from the poor men."

The Nye Committee Hearings proved that Congress already considered our participation in the Second World War an inevitability as early as 1935, although we were supposedly at peace with the world.

Mr. Baruch also stated that:

"Money would be mobilized the same as men and materials, because a price would be fixed at which money could and should be used. I was one of the first who suggested the fixing of prices in the World War, but I do not think you can fix prices and distribution in peacetime."

It may now begin to dawn what all this has to do with the Federal Reserve System. The Federal Reserve System is a central bank whose biggest job is war finance. Its connection with Wall Street brings us back to the public career of Herbert Lehman.

Mayor and Babette (Neugass) Lehman had three sons. Arthur went to Harvard, Irving went to Columbia, and Herbert went to Williams. When they finished college, they entered the family banking house of Lehman Brothers, New York, where they learned the intricacies of world finance, in which their firm played such an important part. Herbert learned, for instance, that the Russian economy was the economy of the future, and he learned that the American economy needed a lot of the improvements they were developing in Russia. Herbert Lehman now has more than twenty years of public srevice behind him.

He was a Colonel on the Army's General Staff during the First World War, a strange place to find a man who had had no military training or experience. He was Lieutenant-Governor and Governor of New York, Military Governor of Italy in 1944 and 1945, head of the United Nations Rehabilitation and Relief Association after the Second World War, and presently Senator of the United States from New York.

"Who's Who in American Jewry" for the year 1928 lists Herbert Lehman as a director of many important corporations, a partial list of which is given here:

Abraham & Straus Department Store (a Rothschild enterprise);

County Trust Company of New York; Jewel Tea Company; Van Raalte Company; Kelsey-Hayes Wheel Company; Pierce Oil Corporation; Spear Company; Studebaker Corporation; Franklin Simon Company; Robert Reis and Company; General American Investors, Limited; Knott Hotels; Fidelity Trust Company; and vice-president of the Palestine Economic Corporation, organized for the industrial development of Palestine. In this work he has been helped most by Edmund M. M. Warburg, director of the Jewish Telegraphic Agency, and General Chairman of the United Jewish Appeal.

In 1939, Congressman Jerry Voorhis of California had begun to ask questions as to why the Government didn't own the Federal Reserve Banks. According to his autobiography, Roosevelt asked him to come over to the White House, and they talked, and Roosevelt said that it seemed to him that it was time they got around to taking over those Federal Reserve Banks, which were now worth $45 billion, as compared to the $143 million they had started with.

The next day Roosevelt's secretary called Jerry Voorhis and told him he had better forget about that conversation, because they would *not* be able to do it for awhile.

The trouble was that the second World War was coming up, and we needed that privately owned central bank to take care of financing the war. Einzig remarks, in "World Finance, 1939-40," Macmillan's, that:

"The transition from 'peace finance' to 'war finance', in comparison with the hurried change of 1914, was carried through in 1939 without any major disturbances."

During the period from 1942 to 1945 the Federal Reserve increased its holdings of Government securities by $22 billion. In other words, its assets doubled during the Second World War, a fortuitous circumstance.

There were no major disturbances because the years between the two World Wars had been years during which the great central banks secured and consolidated control of the world's money and credit. The Federal Reserve System had wiped out all opposition in the Great Depression, and there were numerous organizations which facilitated exchange of information and cooperation between the central banks. First there was the League Finance Committee of the League of Nations, then there was the Bank for International Settlements at Basle, Switzerland, more popularly known as "the central bankers' club", and there were the periodic Economic Conferences at which the central bankers gathered to discuss their control of the world.

During American participation in the Second World War, the Federal Reserve System, besides its normal duties of war finance, took on several new totalitarian controls, one of the most important being the administration of consumer credit, that is, deciding what the worker can spend his salary on.

Governor Marriner Eccles testified at the Senate Hearings on the Office of Price Administration in 1941 that:

"The Federal Reserve Board has acted in consultation with Mr. Henderson's staff. (Leon Henderson, government economist, was appointed by Roosevelt as head of the Office of Price Administration during the war.) He is greatly interested in this question of consumer credit for the reason that *control of the consumer installment credit is a very important power to the principal control of credit.* During the last war there was a shortage of funds, and all during that war we were tied to a gold standard to such an extent that we let the gold standard determine our ability to finance. We have learned a good deal since. When the war was over, the Federal Reserve System forced a contraction of credit through a monetary policy (causing the Aggricultural Depression of 1920-21), which, of course, could not do other than force a great sale of Government securities (at this point discussion off the record, as it frequently was when certain financial matters were being discussed). *You have to protect the market price of Government securities.* The interest rate and the money market are artificial things. New York is the only money market you have.

MR. SMITH: The cost of the gold purchases is not reflected anywhere in the books of the Treasury, so that it enters directly into the public debt structure?

ECCLES: That is correct.

MR. PATMAN: Governor Eccles, when did the Federal Reserve System start charging the Government agencies a service charge?

ECCLES: I really could not say.

MR. PATMAN: Wasn't it intended when the Federal Reserve Act was passed that the Federal Reserve bank would render this service without charge—since under the Act the Government would give them the use of the Government's credit free?

ECCLES: I wouldn't think so."

Emmanuel Goldenweiser writes of the Board during this time: "During the war, quantitative controls were abandoned in order to support government finance." That is, war finance.

The Second World War also gave the big bankers who owned the Federal Reserve System a chance to unload on the country billions of dollars printed early in 1930, in the biggest counterfeiting operation in history, all legalized by Roosevelt's government, of course. Henry Hazlitt writes in the January 4, 1943 issue of Newsweek Magazine:

"The money that began to appear in circulation a week ago, December 21, 1942, was really printing press money in the fullest sense of the term, that is, money which has *no collateral of any kind behind it.* The Federal Reserve statement that 'The Board of Governors, after consultation with the Treasury Department, has authorized Federal Reserve Banks to utilize at this time the existing stocks of currency printed in the early thirties, known as 'Federal Reserve Banknotes'. We repeat, these notes have absolutely no collateral of any kind behind them.''

Governor Eccles also testified to some other interesting matters of the Federal Reserve and war finance at the Senate Hearings on the Office of Price Administration in 1944:

"The currency in circulation was increased from seven billion dollars in four years to twenty-one and a half billion. We are losing some considerable amounts of gold during the war period. As our exports have gone out, largely on a lend-lease basis, we have taken imports on which we have given dollar balances. These countries are now drawing off these dollar balances in the form of gold.

MR. SMITH: Governor Eccles, what is the objective that the foreign governments are after in this projected program whereby we would contribute gold to an international fund?

GOVERNOR ECCLES: I would like to discuss OPA, and leave the stabilization fund for a time when I am prepared to go into it.

MR. SMITH: Just a minute. I feel that this fund is very pertinent to what we are talking about today.

MR. FORD: I believe that the stabilization fund is entirely off the OPA and consequently we ought to stick to the business at hand.''

The Congressmen never did get to discuss the Stabilization Fund, another setup whereby we would give the impoverished countries of Europe back the gold which had been sent over here. In 1945, Henry Hazlitt, commenting, in Newsweek of January 22, on Roosevelt's annual budget message to Congress, quoted Roosevelt as saying:

"I shall later recommend legislation reducing the present high gold reserve requirements of the Federal Reserve Banks.'' Hazlitt pointed out that the reserve requirement was not high, it was just what it had been for the past thirty years. Roosevelt's purpose was to free more gold from the Federal Reserve System and make it available for the Stabilization Fund, later called the International Monetary Fund, part of the World Bank for Reconstruction and Development, the equivalent of the League Finance Committee which would have swallowed the financial sovereignty of the United States if the Senate had let us join it. Consequently, the American people suffered the Great Depression as a result of not joining the League of Nations.

Chapter Fifteen

THOMAS B. McCABE

Immediately after the Second World War, Governor Marriner Eccles began agitating to get back under the control of the Federal Reserve System the 160 billion dollars worth of short-term Government securities, the war bonds purchased by the war workers and soldiers. At the Bretton Woods Hearings on the establishment of the International Monetary Fund, Eccles said:

"The way we financed the war resulted in too much bank financing. The Federal Reserve has to stand ready to purchase these short-term Government securities (war bonds) at the established rate. The option is in the hands of the banks to provide themselves with reserves by selling short-term securities. *That is why increased control by our central bank is necessary.* The option or control over the monetization of the national debt is going to be in the hands of private banks unless it is again restored to the central banking authorities of the Federal Reserve System. You cannot deal with this through the usual orthodox means of raising the rate through open market operations. I think that management of the credit structure is a minor factor in preventing inflation. We must have this International Monetary Fund. *An international currency is synonymous with international government.*"

What Governor Eccles feared was that the banks outside of the Federal Reserve System now had the same opportunities of creating money which had been reserved by the central Federal Reserve Banks, the privilege of creating money by creating reserves when they sold the short-term Government securities, the war bonds issued during the Second World War. How this is done is best revealed by Governor Eccles at Hearings before the House Committee on Banking and Currency on June 24, 1941:

ECCLES: "The banking system as a whole creates and extinguishes the deposits as they make loans and investments, whether they buy Government Bonds or whether they buy utility bonds, or whether they make Farmers' loans.

MR. PATMAN: I am thoroughly in accord with what you say, Governor, but the fact remains that they created the money, did they not?

ECCLES: Well, the banks create money when they make loans and investments."

On September 30, 1941, before the same Committee, Governor Eccles was asked by Representative Patman:

"How did you get the money to buy those two billion dollars worth of Government securities in 1933?

ECCLES: We created it.

MR. PATMAN: Out of what?

ECCLES: Out of the right to issue credit money.

MR. PATMAN: And there is nothing behind it, is there, except our Government's credit?

ECCLES: That is what our money system is. If there were no debts in our money system, there wouldn't be any money."

On June 17, 1942, Governor Eccles was interrogated by Mr. Dewey.

ECCLES: "I mean the Federal Reserve, when it carries out an open market operation, that is, if it purchases Government securities in the open market, it puts new money into the hands of the banks which creates idle deposits.

DEWEY: There are no excess reserves to use for this purpose?

ECCLES: Whenever the Federal Reserve System buys Government securities in the open market, or buys them direct from the Treasury, either one, that is what it does.

DEWEY: What are you going to use to buy them with? You are going to create credit?

ECCLES: That is all we have ever done. That is the way the Federal Reserve System operates. The Federal Reserve System creates money. It is a bank of issue."

At the House Hearings of 1947, Mr. Kilburn asked Mr. Eccles: "What do you mean by monetization of the public debt?

ECCLES: I mean the bank creating money by the purchase of Government securities. All money is created by debt—either private or public debt.

FLETCHER: Chairman Eccles, when do you think there is a possibility of returning to a free and open market, instead of this pegged and artificially controlled financial market we now have?

ECCLES: Never. Not in your lifetime or mine."

We have to have an artificially controlled market because the big bankers do not wish the power of creating money to pass out of their hands. These hearings demonstrate the way that banks can create money if they have quantities of these Government short-term securities or war bonds which were sold during the war. The bankers never intended that the people should get their money back on those bonds. Eccles' group wanted the monetization of the public debt stopped by the exercise of a financial dictatorship which would forbid banks to sell these war bonds and create money by doing so. This would be in keeping with the desires of the International Monetary Fund. Like his dead master, Roosevelt, Eccles was an ardent internationalist. His methods of controlling the 160 billion dollars of money floating around was contrary to President Truman's gang, so Eccles was deprived of the Chairmanship of the Federal Reserve Board of Governors and replaced by Thomas B. McCabe, head of the Toilet-Paper Trust, the Scott Paper Company. McCabe, according to Drew Pearson, had agreed to go along with the Truman-Snyder crowd, who had decided to wipe out the 160 billion dollars of war bonds owned by citizens and banks outside the Federal Reserve System by a very simple method, inflation. Subsidies of farm products and other commodities were increased by the Truman Administration, which since 1945 has steadily followed an inflation policy for the purpose of extinguishing that part of the national debt owed *to* American citizens.

Like Thomas D. Jones in 1914 and Eugene Meyer, Jr. in 1931, Thomas B. McCabe had a very bad record for a man who was to be given supreme financial authority over the American people. He had been President of the Scott Paper Company until 1945, when he was appointed head of the Foreign Liquidation Commission, which disposed of twelve billion dollars worth of surplus Army goods stored abroad. Practically all of those goods found their way into the black markets of the world, or were sold by black market methods by McCabe's assistants. The industrialists did not care what he did with the stuff. They had been paid for it, the bill was now part of the national debt, and all McCabe had to do was to be sure that it did not get back into the United States and compete with the post-war production. He could give it away sell it, anything to get it off the market.

The Senate Hearings proved conclusively that Thomas B. McCabe was directly responsible for the black market dealings carried out by men under his immediate supervision. One of the more unsavory of such incidents was McCabe's officer in charge of surplus stored in China selling blood plasma, (which had been donated by loyal Americans to the troops who were fighting overseas) on the Chinese black market. The enterprising Chinese advertised it in their newspapers, being careful to point out to prospective purchasers that it was *American* blood. The Hearings also brought out the interesting fact that large quantities of narcotics, chiefly morphine and codeine from first-aid kits, went from McCabe's Foreign Liquidation Commission directly into international narcotics trade.

These billions of dollars worth of Army material which were being given away or sold for a fraction of their worth, had a very corrupting influence on the domestic politics of countries where there were large depots of such supplies. Particularly in England, China, India, and the Phillippine Islands did the Foreign Liquidation Commission encourage criminal activity among politicians which, six years later, is still bringing to light unsavory incidents.

Walter B. Schleiter, employee of Muller-Phipps Asia Ltd., New York, export-import merchants dealing with China and India, had been one of McCabe's agents in India. He got into trouble because he tried to be honest, and attempted to keep open bids on the merchandise which he was charged with disposing of. A British firm, represented by Sir Archibald Rowlandson, had already made an agreement over Schleiter's head to buy this merchandise at their own price, and Schleiter was sent home. He told the following amusing anecdote at the Senate Hearings on Thomas B. McCabe.

SENATOR TOBEY, CHAIRMAN: That is the figure, three hundred million dollars, that you accuse Sir Archibald Rowlandson of stealing from you, facetiously?

SCHLEITER: That was more or less humorous.

TOBEY: But it is a grim joke, accusing a man of stealing three hundred million dollars from you.

SCHLEITER: That is what I thought he had done. And he more or less admitted it, Senator.

TOBEY: Did he?

SCHLEITER: He did.

TOBEY: Did he pay for the lunch?

SCHLEITER: He paid for the drink."

Despite these revelations of unbelievable corruption, officially involving a high Government agency, the Foreign Liquidation Commission, with deals in narcotic smuggling and selling American blood on the Chinese black market, the Senate approved of the fact that Thomas B. McCabe had gotten rid of twelve billion dollars worth of Army surplus on the black markets of the world, and confirmed his appointment by President Truman as Chairman of the Board of Governors of the Federal Reserve System.

Thomas B. McCabe now issued a statement that:

"Our basic problem is to absorb reserves in the Federal Reserve System."

This was an oversimplification of the problem. The reserves, in the first place, which he wished to absorb, were outside of the jurisdiction of the System. The Administration had to extinguish them by encouraging high prices. Thus, the amount of currency, the printing press Federal Reserve notes without any collateral behind them, which by any name meant counterfeit, had swollen from seven billion dollars in 1940 to twenty-one and a half billion dollars in 1944, had shrunk after the war, and by spring of 1951 had been swollen again to more than twenty-seven billion dollars, to increase inflation and wipe out that part of the debt owed to the loyal workers and soldiers who had been cajoled and threatened into buying war bonds during the war. The Federal Reserve had to play second fiddle to John Snyder and the United States Treasury in the handling of this outstanding credit. Meanwhile, the Treasury was spending billions of dollars to keep up the price of these short-term Government securities on the exchange, in order to protect the big speculators like Baruch and Lehman who owned most of them.

Eccles' last plea for power in the Federal Reserve System through dictatorial methods in handling this free credit had been made at the House Hearings on the continuance of the Office of Price Administration in 1946, when he said:

"Our money supply expands through borrowing. The Government can stop further creation of bank credit by bringing about a balanced budget. It could reduce the existing supply of money by paying down the public debt and have commercial banks sell some of their Government securities to nonbank investors (charitable and educational foundations). Stopping further monetization of the public debt will tend to stabilize interest rates."

This statement was in direct contradiction to the wishes of the crowd backing Truman and Snyder. They wanted further monetization of the debt as an integral part of their inflation policy, and they most emphatically did not wish to pay down the public debt. With five billions of dollars a year in interest coming in, what banker would wish to pay down the public debt?

At the House Committee on Banking and Currency Hearings February 21, 1945, on the extension of the public debt, Undersecretary of the Treasury Bell read a prepared statement saying that the public debt of the United States then amounted to 232 billion dollars. Mr. Jenkins of Ohio protested that the actual debt was at least a hundred billion dollars more than that. Mr. William Lemke of North Dakota figured that, considering the total long term commitments of the government, the debt amounted to *643 billion dollars*, a figure which has not yet been successfully disputed.

In answer to Mr. Jenkins' protest about a mere hundred billion dollars, Undersecretary Bell said:

"Oh, you must be including 67 to 68 billion dollars of unliquidated obligations under contracts entered into by various departments of the Government." The unliquidated obligations, as Undersecretary Bell finally admitted, were debts.

Then Secretary of the Treasury Fred Vinson, speaking at the Bretton Woods Hearings before the House Committee in May, 1946, spoke of Britain's First World War debt, incurred through the ministrations of Ambassador Walter Hines Page, J. P. Morgan Company, and Woodrow Wilson:

"Her first war debt was four and a quarter billion dollars, of which she paid about two billion, of which 450 million dollars was principal, and one billion six hundred million was interest." The significiance of these figures should not be lost. The principal was owed to the American people, through the proceeds of Liberty Loans. The interest was paid to international bankers. Three-fourths of her total repayment went to bankers in the form of interest, one-fourth came back to our Treasury, and more than half of the total debt was repudiated in its entirety by the British Government.

Secretary Vinson, later Chief Justice of the Supreme Court, also testified at the Bretton Woods Hearings that:

"One reason we did not accept the Clearing Union was that it permitted credit creation. The Bretton Woods Plan was quite different. I was there helping make it. The idea of creating credit was rejected by the International Bank."

The International Bank for Reconstruction and Development, headed by Eugene Meyer, Jr., and the International Monetary Fund, were created to extinguish the enormous amount of credit created by the Second World War After the First World War, we had two great depressions to extinguish the credit produced by the war. The totalitarian dictatorship of these organizations, taking over the sovereignty and the right to coin money of every country in the world, should make depressions unnessary.

Governor Eccles had remarked before the Senate Committee that:

"An international currency is synonymous with international government."

The League of Nations had failed because it had not created an international currency. It had not been able to do so because it had failed to enlist the credit of the Government of the United States behind it, and we had the Great Depression of 1929-31 as the inevitable result of that condition.

Colonel Ely Garrison, in his book, "Roosevelt, Wilson, and the Federal Reserve Act", published in 1915, had pointed out that:

"In finance, there can be no doubt about the stabilizing influence of internationalism, whereby closely knit alliances of money groups and forces in scattered sections of the world can come to the relief of their beleaguered friends."

Essentially, this internationalism means making the people of one country responsible for debts of another country. Through central banks, the big bankers have organized the credit of entire countries, and through alliances of central banks, they have organized the credit of groups of countries. Through the creation of enormous and inextinguishable debts, they now propose to rule unchallenged over all peoples of the world.

Phillips, in his textbook, "Readings in Money and Banking", said:

"The banker, relatively speaking, has no human factor to consider."

Henry Hazlitt, in Newsweek of August 16, 1948, said:

"The world dollar shortage will last as long as world exchange control lasts. And the American taxpayer will continue to foot the bill."

We can thank Eugene Meyer, Jr. and the International Monetary Fund for that. Young pointed out in the American Economic Review of September, 1947, that:

"The International Monetary Fund provided for revision of rates, but only on the event of fundamental disequilibrium. The day of fluctuating rates is gone. Rates now *a matter of considered decision* to a degree greater than ever before."

Fundamental disequilibrium, of course, meant any time the people might get hold of their own money, as after the Second War when they had that purchasing power held in the war bonds which they had bought.

R. S. Sayers, in the Quarterly Journal of Economics of May, 1949, gives a clear summation of the aims of the Federal Reserve System since the end of the war. He says:

"The latest decades have been a consolidation of the power of the world's greatest central banks, the Federal Reserve System, and the Bank of England—of their power, that is to say, to control their respective monetary systems. The Governors of the Federal Reserve Board, however, are not satisfied by the great extension of their power over the total supply of money. Among the newer powers they have been persistently seeking from Congress are a freer hand in the alteration of cash reserve rations, and the power to prescribe minimum rations of short-term government paper to be held by the commercial banks. Although the latter proposal found its origin in the particular shape of postwar bank statistics, it is fundamentally to be ascribed to the Reserve Board of Governors' desire to secure complete control over the quantity and price of credit. The swing of opinion is away from a simple quantitative control of credit, such as was given by the original Federal Reserve Act of 1913, and the desire of the Federal Reserve System for permanent powers on the lines of the wartime emergency powers, to regulate installment credit, is in substantial alignment with Governor Eccles' ideas on consumer credit control and the regulation of house-purchase finance, although central bank action in this field could hardly be necessary where government subsidies were important and could be varied as a part of general employment policy."

Eccles was as power mad as his mentor Roosevelt. He sought to maintain the dictatorial consumer credit controls and to secure for the Board of Governors power in the home finance field, in which the United States already was operating a substantial monopoly.

Representative H. O. Talle of Ohio pointed out that:

"If a central bank has in mind control of credit, as we had in our Federal Reserve System when we employed the rediscount rate and open market operations, and as when the government operates on a cheap money policy, the central bank of the government is thwarted in its attempt to control credit and stabilize the price level. Our money system and our banking system are the same. We are slaves to our public debt."

The 643 billion dollars of public debt is the controlling factor in America's financial system, and the Federal Reserve Board has managed it as a central bank manages a debt, that is, the Government's credit is now mortgaged to them, and there is no way under the present monetary system whereby the credit of the people of the United States can ever become their rightful property once more.

Edward C. Simmons said in the American Economic Review of September, 1947:

"There can be no doubt that the twelve Federal Reserve Banks and the coordinating machinery represented by the Board of Governors and the Open Market Committee constitute a central bank which has been erected to make the volume of the mass of payment a manageable variable."

This is a more complicated way of saying, "control of money and credit."

C. R. Whittlesey of the University of Pennsylvania said before the American Economic Association in 1944:

"Bank loans have changed from commercial loans to comprise substantial amounts of collateral, real estate, term, and personal loans. They have very largely ceased to be commmercial in origin or self-liquidating in character. In addition, income from services, particularly in service charges on checking accounts, has come to play an appreciable part in bank emolument. A second major change in banking has been the emergence on a large scale of excess reserves, and their continuance year after year in spite of strong efforts to reduce them. While excess reserves have existed for short periods in the past, notably after the establishment of the Federal Reserve System, this constitutes a distinct departure from accepted banking tradition. Keynes laid down the law that reserves must be used to the hilt. Other changes involve establishment of the Federal Deposit Insurance Corporation, adoption by the Federal Reserve Board of an active policy with respect to government bonds, and to the pattern of interest rates."

Whittlesey's survey of the changes in the character of banking point up the most important factor, the lessening and almost disappearance of banking's oldest and primary function, lending money to start businesses and aid in production, loans which were self-liquidating in character. In the first place, the giant trusts established during and after the Great Depression of 1929-31, controlled and financed themselves from their own treasuries any further business expansion in this country, so that avenue of investment was closed to banks. It was to the bankers' own interest, however, to change the nature of their loans from self-liquidating to inextinguishable debts, as the following quotation from Henry Ford makes apparent:

"The one aim of these financiers is world control by the creation of inextinguishable debts. And since gold is a metal which neither laws or inventions can increase, the supplies of which Nature has so far limited, control has become a very simple achievement."

Since the end of the Second World War, there has sprung up a world-wide black market in gold, in which the Federal Reserve System, as the world's largest holder of gold, and the United States Government, which has pegged the price of gold at $35 an ounce, are inextricably involved. Our Government is selling gold at $35 an ounce to black marketeers who retail it from $57 to $75 an ounce anywhere in the world. The Gold Trading Act of 1949, which sought to restore a free market in gold, was opposed by our Government because the United States is controlled by these international gold dealers and black marketeers. Some of the Hearings on this Act are given below:

Mr. Lawrence, banker from New York, said:

"Aramco (Arabian-American Oil Company) made a deal with Ibn Saud agreeing to give him, among other things, 80 million dollars in British gold sovereigns. The earth was scoured in order to find the eighty million dollars in British sovereigns. And you may be surprised, gentlemen, just as much as I was, to know that these eighty million dollars in British gold sovereigns were finally found to be in the possession of a gentleman named Peron. A deal was made, and an additional twenty million dollars in British gold sovereigns was provided, which is being used today for purposes which I cannot exactly define, in Greece. We, who are in possession of 75 percent of the world's gold, are forced to go to South America and make a deal under the counter, paying fifty to sixty dollars an ounce, as compared to our own thirty-five dollars an ounce set by Mr. Roosevelt. Is it not strange that we are forced in an important deal of this kind to go to Peron and obtain from him on terms we cannot exactly ascertain at the present time, an amount of gold sufficient to perform a simple contract like this? The free gold market in this country from 1862-1879 or the free gold market prevailing in Great Britain from 1919-1925 did not create any currency chaos. *During the war and postwar years the moneys of the world have been in the hands of men who believed in a managed currency.* The originator of this theory is Georg Friederich Knapp. This man, in the time of the Kaiser, believed that a state could give its currency any value that it chose. He outlined for the first time the complex structure of exchange controls later adopted by Schacht in Nazi Germany. This same theory was given a slightly different angle and sold to the Anglo-Saxon world by Lord Keynes. A managed currency in this country means that Congress must forfeit its constitutional power to regulate the value of money and delegate it to a non-elected and politically irresponsible bureaucracy. The men who make up our Federal Reserve Board and the International Monetary Fund are not men who have to face the approval or disapproval of an electorate. Largely as a result of English influence, this country organized the Betton Woods institutions, the International Monetary Fund and the World Bank for Reconstruction and Development. Out of a total fund capital of eight billion dollars, this country contributed two billion seven hundred and fifty million in gold.

CHAIRMAN: We have put up all the gold?

MR. LAWRENCE: Yes."

At these same hearings, Mr. Searles, President of the Newmont

Mining Company, gave for the first time the story behind the dramatic airlift operation in Berlin.

MR. SEARLES: "I have figured for the price of the airlift. It cost 350 million dollars. Now, if we had put 350 million dollars in gold behind the mark currency of Berlin, we would not have had to have that airlift. The cause of the airlift and the Russian blockade into Berlin was the dispute over the Berlin currency and the introduction of the Deutsch-mark. And the failure of the United Nations to end that blockade last autumn, if you remember, was due to the fact that the *United Nations would not permit a sufficient length of time to negotiate over the Berlin currency.* I once wrote Sproul of the Federal Reserve Board and said if this government would permit the export of newly mined gold, it would swamp the black market in gold in a short time."

The international gold merchants do not want a free market in gold, and so the United States Government does not want a free market in gold.

Seltzer said before the American Economic Association in 1946 that:

"Since 1929 our commercial banking system has been transformed from one in which bank deposits and bank earnings were based mainly on direct customer loans to one in which they earn money mainly from bank ownership of the public debt." The commercial banks' enormous income from the ownership of the public debt and subsequent lack of interest in loans has given rise to the small loan companies which charge exorbitant rates of interest, and to the auto loan and finance companies which charge extremely high rates.

H. A. Dulan in the Southwestern Quarterly of June, 1943, says: "Prior to 1943, member banks of the Federal Reserve System relied on interest and discount on loans for the largest portion of their earnings. Since 1943, the interest and dividends on securities from the public debt have contributed the largest portion of earnings."

Besides important bankers, appointments to the Federal Reserve Board lately have included big industrialists such as Ernest G. Draper, President of the big California packers, Hill Brothers, and Dromedary Date Company, and Thomas B. McCabe, head of the Toilet-Paper Trust, the Scott Paper Company. In March, 1951, McCabe resigned as Chairman of the Federal Reserve Board of Governors, and was replaced by William McChesney Martin, former President of the Stock Exchange, and former President of the Export-Import Bank. Martin's father was a close associate of Paul Warburg in the American Acceptance Council, and worked with him to get American finance and industry to adopt the use of acceptances, on which Warburg held a virtual monopoly in this country.

The elder Martin was Governor of the Federal Reserve Bank of St. Louis.

Whatever its leadership, the Federal Reserve Board is committed to tightening its financial supremacy over the United States. Bernard Baruch testified before Congress that:

"We have not had a free or competitive economy since the First World War."

Governor Marriner Eccles testified that we should not see our money market free from the money power's control in our lifetime.

The latest statement was made by Governor Mencius Szymczak of the Federal Reserve Board, who was appointed by Boss Kelly of Chicago to that office. Governor Szymczak stated in Time Magazine in September, 1950, that:

"The more we can accomplish by means of monetary, credit, and fiscal policies, the less need there will be for the authoritarian harness of rationing and other direct controls."

The most ominous pronouncement of the real rulers of the country, the trust owners who control finance and business, comes from Peter Drucker, a spokesman for them. Writing in the Saturday Evening Post of October 28, 1944, on the occasion of the Bretton Woods agreements, Mr. Drucker wrote:

"Should the world adopt a controlled economic system, leadership would logically fall to the Soviet Union. Russia would be the model for such a dictatorship, for Russia was the first country to develop the technique of international economic control—for transacting monopoly directed foreign trade and foreign exchange money. Her independence and military success had shown us naturally what could be done with such policies, which explains the acceptance of these policies by independent labor unions and political parties the world over."

In the first place, Russia has no independence, as far as her citizens are concerned. In the second place, as a military success she collapsed when Hitler marched against Moscow, and was saved only by American production and shipment of lend-lease supplies given by our people. Nevertheless, our trust-owners whole-heartedly admire the way Stalin and the Politburo have subjected the Russian people to their dictatorship, and our own versions of Stalin and the Politburo are well on their way to doing the same thing over here.

This dictatorship cannot be exercised without the control of money and credit. If Congress actually had retained its sovereignty and refused to let Woodrow Wilson and Carter Glass hand over the sovereign right of coinage and the issue of our money to private bankers in 1913, the American people today would not stand on the brink of slavery. The Federal Reserve System has been the death of our Constitution. The Federal Reserve Board of Governors, chosen by and working for the powerful international bankers, have inflicted catastrophe after castastrophe upon our people. They have involved us into two World Wars, they have planned and executed two of the worst economic depressions we have ever suffered. The American people have been kept in ignorance of the forces working against them. The love of liberty, the innate self-reliance, and the uncompromising individualism of the native American must assert itself against the control of the Federal Reserve Board if we are to renew the American Republic.

BIBLIOGRAPHY OF "THE FEDERAL RESERVE"

Poor's Directory of Directors, Standard and Poor Publishing Corp. Volumes referred to from 1928 to 1951.
Who's Who In America, A. N. Marquis Co. Volumes referred to from 1896 to 1951.
The Federal Reserve System, by Paul Moritz Warburg, MacMillan, 1930.
The Federal Reserve System, by H. Parker Willis, Ronald Co., 1923.
A B C of the Federal Reserve System, by E. W. Kemmerer, Princeton University Press, 1919.
Adventure In Constructive Finance, by Carter Glass, Doubleday, 1927.
U. S. Federal Reserve Board Bulletins. Volumes referred to from 1914 to 1951.
U. S. Federal Reserve Board Annual Reports. Volumes referred to from 1914 to 1950.
Banking Reform in the United States, by Paul Moritz Warburg, Academy of Political Science, Columbia University, July, 1914.
Senate Committee Hearings on Federal Reserve Act, 1913.
House Committee Hearings on Federal Reserve Act, 1913.
House Committee Hearings on the Money Trust (Pujo Commmittee) 1913.
House Investigation of Federal Reserve System, 1927-1928.
Senate Investigation on Fitness of Eugene Meyer to be a Governor of the Federal Reserve Board, 1930.
Senate Hearings on Office of Price Administration, 1941.
House Report on Nomination of Thomas D. Jones to be a Governor of the Federal Reserve Board, 1914.
Senate Hearings on Office of Price Administration, 1944.
Senate Hearings on Thomas B. McCabe to be a Governor of the Federal Reserve System, 1948.
House Committee Hearings on Extension of Public Debt, 1945.
Who's Who In American Jewry, 1926-1939.

APPENDIX I TO SECOND EDITION

One of the most respected Wall Street economists recently remarked that "The central bank, of course, was devised to get us off of the hook of the gold standard." The gold standard long ago was proved to be inadequate for modern commerce, since insufficient currency or credits could be issued on a strict adherence to the gold standard to finance the development of industrial civilization. The international elements who controlled the gold standard realized that unless they came up with a suitable alternative, they would have to abandon the gold standard, and with it their enormous political and economic power. The central bank was that alternative.

By the hocus-pocus of reserves, central banks were able to increase their issue of currency and credits by many times. When securities were made the basis of monetary issue, enormous pyramiding of paper credits became possible, and speculators were able to erect fantastic financial houses of cards, which, of course, collapsed in due time, bringing the inevitable losses to investors. These abuses led directly to the debacle of 1929, with the active participation of the Federal Reserve Board of Governors. The collapse of world economy which occurred then has remained largely unalleviated, except for stopgap financial measures.

The future of long-term bond financing at this writing is extremely dubious. Since the central bankers have pyramided the system of national debts past the point where they can possibly be repaid, they are assets only because of the yearly interest collected. The central bankers are desperately trying to maintain an economic status quo and continue to collect that interest. They are collecting five billion dollars a year in interest on the public debt of the United States Government, a sum larger than the entire postwar debt of the German nation. This interest of course is more important than the astronomical and uncollectible principal. This five billion dollars a year is the rent which the central bankers are charging the American people for the use of America's credit during the Second World War.

The central bankers have tried to protect their interests by internationalizing their system of astronomical public debts, and by making the only financially sound nation, the United States, responsible for bankrupt European states. This was done by setting up the International Monetary Fund at Bretton Woods in 1944. Henry Hazlitt wrote in Newsweek Magazine, Dec. 31, 1951, that "The chief remaining obstacle to a world restoration of freedom and sound money is the International Monetary Fund, an unnecessary institution set up, under the influence of the late Lord Keynes and Harry Dexter White, on a completely unsound basis."

The architect of the International Fund was Harry Dexter White, son of Lithuanian Jewish immigrants and one of the three most important Communist spies in America. With him at Bretton Woods were Frank Coe, Lauchlin Currie, William L. Ullmann, and Nathan Silvermaster. All of these men have been identified as Communist traitors. President Truman appointed White as director of the International Monetary Fund AFTER the FBI informed him of White's Communist background. Currie had been personal assistant to Franklin Roosevelt during the Second World War. Currie, Hiss, White, and Coe enjoyed direct Presidential immunity from exposure of their Communist treason.

Currie and White were monetary experts, bent on wrecking the last free economy of the world, the American free enterprise economy. The reader may well wonder how international banking has been so closely tied up with Communism, which advertises itself as the enemy of bankers. Actually, Communism is the last reaction of an outmoded system of gold standard banking, financed and politically aided by those bankers, to the extent that when the German armies threatened this institution of Communism, the American nation was sent out to save Communism from extinction, by the great crusader, Franklin D. Roosevelt.

The American people have assumed the burden of hundreds of billions of dollars of debt simply because we let a handful of enemy aliens take over our monetary system. The three most important architects of our present monetary system are almost completely unknown to the average American citizen, who pays a heavy annual rate of taxation because of their machinations.

They are Paul Warburg, the German Jew who wrote the Federal Reserve Act, Emmanuel Goldenweiser, the Russian Jew who supervised the details of Federal Reserve Board operations through its first thiry years, and Harry Dexter White, son of Lithuanian Jews, who set up the International Monetary Fund. Paul Warburg was one of the financiers of the Communist revolution in Russia, and Harry Dexter White was a key man in the Communist conspiracy here in America.

According to the obituary of Dr. Goldenweiser in the New York Times, April 6, 1953, Elliott Thurston, Governor of the Federal Reserve Board, said on Dr. Goldenweiser's retirement in 1945 that "He undoubtedly has contributed more, over a longer period of time, to important policy-making in the Federal Government than any other civil servant."

Yet what American citizen ever heard of Dr. Goldenweiser? Who had heard of Harry Dexter White, whose machinations cost us hundreds of millions of dollars in Germany after the Second World War when he turned over the U. S. Treasury plates for printing occupation marks to his Communist accomplices? American citizens must reclaim their power of monetary issue from these enemy aliens or endure the collapse of our economy and our Western civilization.

Some brief notes on principal figures in this book are appended:
PAUL WARBURG: Died 1932. His son, James Paul Warburg, whose books are replete with Communist propaganda, was a member of Franklin D. Roosevelt's Brain Trust, propaganda chief of Eisenhower's headquarters in London during the Second World War, mastermind of the Eisenhower Presidential campaign, and chief backer of the United World Federalists, world government movement.

HENRY MORGENTHAU JR: Morgenthau's personal assistant in the U. S. Treasury, Harry Dexter White, was exposed as a principal Communist agent. Morgenthau is now prominent in Zionist activities.

HERBERT LEHMAN: Now a U. S. Senator, Lehman spent hundreds of millions of dollars of American money in Central Europe during the Second World War, as head of United Nations Relief and Rehabilitation Agency. This money was spent to ensure that "reactionary" governments would not come back into power, and that post-war Central Europe would be under the control of "Liberal, democratic" elements, the Communist Party. Lehman's personal assistant, Laurence Duggan, with a long record of fellow-traveling activity, died suddenly the day before he was due to be interrogated by the House Un-American Activities Committee. His intimate friend, Sumner Welles, as well as other government leaders, denied that Duggan had killed himself.

Current Biography notes that Herbert Lehman was elected Governor of New York with the active support of the Communist Party. The chief corporate representative of his family banking house, Lehman Brothers, is General Lucius Clay. One of Eisenhower's closest advisors, Clay was identified in the New York Post, April 19, 1953, as the man who selected George Humphrey as Eisenhower's Secretary of the Treasury.

LEWIS LICHTENSTEIN STRAUSS: Partner of Kuhn, Loeb Co. former private secretary of Herbert Hoover, commissioned as Rear Admiral in World War II, appointed member of first U. S. Atomic Energy Commission by President Truman, appointed personal advisor on atomic energy to President Eisenhower, showing that Kuhn, Loeb Co. is always above partisan politics.

Statement Of Congressman Wright Patman, Of The House Banking And Currency Committee

April 14, 1952, the Board of Governors addressed a letter to me, as chairman of the Subcommittee on General Credit Control and Debt Management of the Joint Committee on the Economic Report, in reply to my letter requesting information, in which the Chairman of the Board stated that he was enclosing a memorandum prepared by the counsel of the Federal Reserve Board concerning the legal status of the Board and the Federal Reserve banks. Of course, this opinoin was also the opinion of the Board of Governors.

Excerpts from the statement are as follows:

STATUS OF THE BOARD OF GOVERNORS OF THE FEDERAL SYSTEM AND OF THE FEDERAL RESERVE BANKS

"The Board of Governors was created by Congress and is a part of the Government of the United States. Its members are appointed by the President, with the advice and consent of the Senate, and it has been held by the Attorney General to be a Government establishment (30 Op. Atty. Gen., 308 (1914).

"The 12 Federal Reserve banks are corporations set up by Federal law to operate for public purposes under Government supervision.

"The Federal Reserve banks derive their existence and powers from statutes passed by Congress, and in this practical sense may be looked upon as agencies of Congress.

"In view of the public nature of their functions, the courts have held the Federal Reserve banks to be agencies or instrumentalities of the Federal Government.

"There is no free market that can cope with a national debt of $272 billion, with $85 billion of it to be refunded within 1 year. Free market means private manipulation of credit. The Federal Reserve Board, to my mind, is guilty of the grossest kind of misconduct in failing to support the Government of the United States at a time of its greatest economic peril in Government securities. As an instrument of the Government, it is itself failing and refusing during a time of need to come to the aid and rescue of the Government and the people.

The Real Power Behind The Throne

"The Open Market Committee of the Federal Reserve System is composed of the 7 members of the Board of Governors and 5 members who are presidents of Federal Reserve banks and who were selected by private commercial banking interests. The Open Market Committee has the power to obtain, and does obtain, the printed money of the United States—Federal Reserve notes—from the Bureau of Engraving and Printing, and exchanges these printed notes, which of course are not interest bearing, for United States Government obligations that are interest bearing. After making the exchange, the interest bearing obligations are retained by the 12 Federal Reserve banks and the interest collected annually on these Government obligations goes into the funds of the 12 Federal Reserve banks. These funds are expended by the system without an adequate accounting to Congress. In fact there has never been an independent audit of either the 12 banks or the Federal Reserve Board that has been filed with the Congress where a Member would have an opportunity to inspect it. The General Accounting Office does not have jurisdiction over the Federal Reserve. For 40 years the system, while freely using money of the Government, has not made a proper accounting.

"The Open Market Committee operation is the most important function of the entire Federal Reserve System. It provides either hard money or easy money. It makes conditions good or bad. It determines whether or not we will have a depression in this country or whether or not our country will remain prosperous."